MW00685412

READER'S DIGEST

GREAT**HEALTHY**COOKING

Fruit Dishes
& Desserts

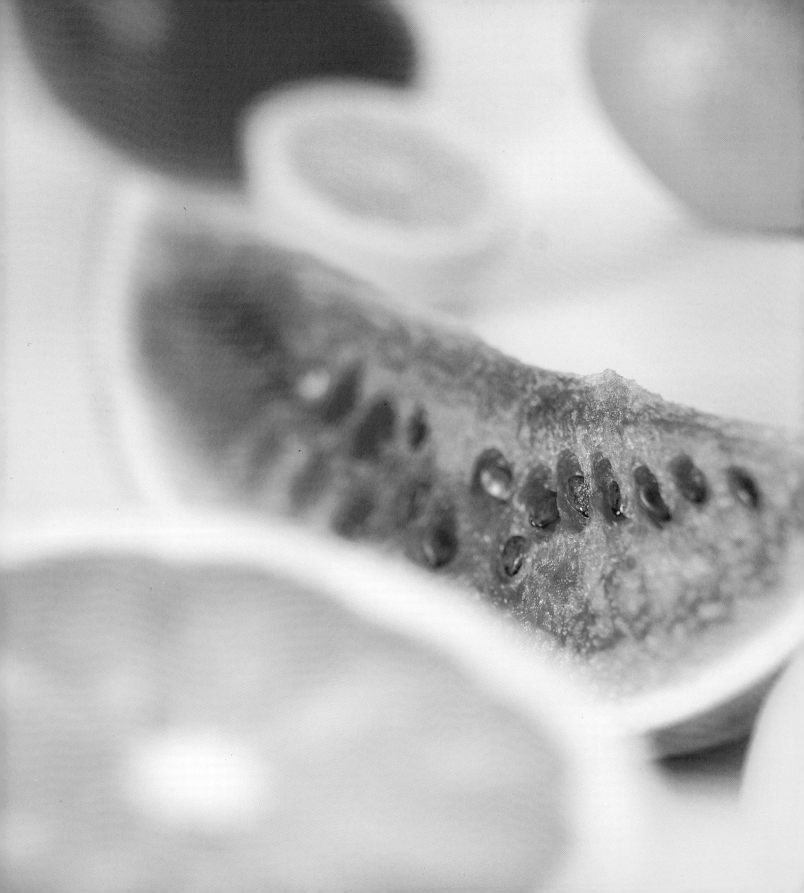

READER'S DIGEST

GREATHEALTHYCOOKING

Fruit Dishes
& Desserts

Reader's
Digest

THE READER'S DIGEST ASSOCIATION, INC.
Pleasantville, New York/Montreal

FRUIT DISHES & DESSERTS is part of a cookbook series called GREAT HEALTHY COOKING.

Editorial Director: Carol A. Guasti
Design Director: Elizabeth Tunnicliffe
Produced by: Beth Allen Associates, Inc.
  President/Editorial Director: Beth Allen
  Art Director: Kathleen McGilvery
  Nutritionist: Michele C. Fisher, Ph.D., R.D.
  Recipe Tester: Lorna Charles
  Recipe Editor: Judith Blahnik
  Copy Editor: Wendy Marcus
Photographers: Sue Atkinson, Martin Brigdale, Gus Filgate, Graham Kirk
Stylists: Sue Russell, Helen Trent

Reader's Digest General Books
Editor-in-Chief: Christopher Cavanaugh
Art Director: Joan Mazzeo

Reader's Digest General Books/United Kingdom
Editorial Director: Cortina Butler
Art Director: Nick Clark
Series Editor: Christine Noble

Library of Congress Cataloging in Publication Data
Fruit dishes & desserts.
        p. cm. -- (Reader's Digest great healthy cooking)
  Includes index.
  ISBN 0-7621-0274-8
  1. Cookery (Fruit) 2. Desserts. I. Reader's Digest Association.
II. Series.
TX811.F765 1999
641.6'4—dc21   99-33599

First Edition Copyright © 1999
The Reader's Digest Association Limited
11 Westferry Circus, Canary Wharf, London E14 4HE

Copyright © 1999 The Reader's Digest Association, Inc.
Copyright © 1999 The Reader's Digest Association (Canada) Ltd.
Copyright © 1999 Reader's Digest Association Far East Limited
Philippine Copyright © 1999 Reader's Digest Association Far East Limited

All rights reserved. No part of this book may be reproduced, stored in a retrieval system or transmitted in any form or by any means, electronic, electrostatic, magnetic tape, mechanical, photocopying, recording or otherwise, without permission in writing from the publishers.

® Reader's Digest, The Digest and the Pegasus logo are registered trademarks of The Reader's Digest Association, Inc, of Pleasantville, New York, USA.

Printed in the United States of America 1999

Notes to the reader

- Recipes were tested using standard measurements by professional recipe testers, to ensure perfect results.
- Conventional ovens, not convection or microwave ovens, were used in the kitchen testing of recipes.
- Large eggs were used.
- Low-fat milk (2% milkfat) was used unless another is specified.
- Can sizes are approximate, as weights can vary slightly according to the manufacturer.
- Preparation and cooking times are intended only as a guide.

The nutritional information in this book is for reference only. Anyone with continuing medical problems or symptoms should consult a doctor.

Contents

6
Introduction
Eating well to live well

8
Super Fruit
10 Fabulous fruits for a healthy diet
14 A new look at favorite fruits
18 Fruits from around the world
22 Concentrated fruity goodness
24 Preparing and cooking fruits
25 Fruit coulis
    Berry coulis
    Blackberry coulis

26
A Great Start
28 Strawberry yogurt smoothie
30 Mango, peach, and apricot fizz
32 Banana and mango shake
34 Citrus wake-up
36 Frozen pineapple and berry slush
38 Apricot-pecan muffins
40 Orchard spread
42 Spicy date, apple, and cheese dip
44 Blueberry and cranberry granola

46
Raw Vitality

48 Berry salad with passion fruit
50 Pimm's melon cup
52 Apple and date salad
54 Watermelon and feta salad
56 Tropical fruit with coriander
58 Citrus and spinach salad

60
Savory Ways with Fruit

62 Thai shrimp and pineapple
64 Chicken with apricots and cumin
66 Lamb and fig stew with star anise
68 Pork chops with Asian pears
70 Prune and prosciutto kebabs with apricot sauce
72 Thai stir-fried steak with mango
74 Roasted roots with apricots
76 *Frijoles* with fruit
78 Pears broiled with pecorino

80
Fast Fruit Desserts

82 Flambéed Asian pears with orange
84 Grilled fruit *en brochettes*
86 Hot apricot soufflés
88 Saffron and vanilla grilled fruit
90 Plums *en papillote* with honey

92 Glazed banana *pain perdu*
94 Peach and blackberry phyllo pizzas
96 Cranberry and banana rice pudding
98 Summer fruit fool
100 Hot plum sauce

102
Sweet Finales

104 Rhubarb and saffron crème brûlée
106 Pear crêpes with chocolate sauce
108 Baked almond-stuffed peaches
110 Cherry brandy clafoutis
112 Steamed kumquat honey pudding
114 Raspberry queen of puddings
116 Pear and blueberry shortbread
118 Plum and marzipan pastries
120 Strawberry cheese tart
122 Black Forest mousse cake
124 Sultana lemon cheesecake
126 Summer pudding
128 Apple crème caramel
130 Frozen raspberry yogurt
132 Tropical trifle
134 Strawberry and cranberry granita
136 Persian almond crème
138 Sweet balsamic berry ice cream

140 A glossary of nutritional terms
142 Index

Eating well to live well

It's no secret: Eating a healthful diet and leading a health-filled lifestyle help you look good, feel great, and have lots of energy. Nutrition fads come and go. But it's a fact that eating well for your health's sake is simple. Eat a variety of foods, because no one food contains all the vitamins, minerals, fiber, and other essential nutrients you need. And get the balance right. This means look at the overall picture of which foods you eat, when you eat them, and how much you eat. And be sure to get exercise along the way.

Getting the balance right!

The Dietary Guidelines for Americans help us to get the balance right by eating a healthy diet. The United States Department of Agriculture (USDA) and the Department of Health and Human Services used the most current scientific information available to develop these guidelines for all Americans (age 2 or older). By following these guidelines, you not only can enjoy better health, but also can reduce your chances for getting certain diseases.

The Dietary Guidelines for Americans

1. *Eat a variety of foods* to get the energy, protein, vitamins, minerals, and fiber you need for good health.
2. *Balance the food you eat with physical activity — maintain or improve your weight* to reduce your chances of high blood pressure, heart disease, certain cancers, and a stroke.
3. *Choose a diet with plenty of grain products, vegetables, and fruits* that provide needed vitamins, minerals, fiber, and complex carbohydrates, and that can help you lower your intake of fat.
4. *Chose a diet low in fat, saturated fat, and cholesterol* to reduce your risk of heart attack and certain types of cancer and to help you maintain a healthy weight.
5. *Choose a diet moderate in sugars.* A high-sugar diet has too many calories and too few nutrients for most people and can contribute to tooth decay. Use that "spoonful of sugar" sparingly!
6. *Choose a diet moderate in salt and sodium* (no more than 2,400mg each day) to help reduce your risk of high blood pressure.
7. *If you drink alcoholic beverages, do so in moderation* (no more than 1 to 2 drinks a day). Alcoholic beverages supply calories but little or no nutrients. Drinking is also the cause of many health problems and accidents, and can lead to addiction.

Putting the Dietary Guidelines into action

By following the Food Guide Pyramid, you put the Dietary Guidelines for Americans into daily action. The Pyramid calls for eating a variety of foods to get the nutrients you need to maintain your health. It's designed to guide you toward a diet that does not have too many calories or too much fat, saturated fat, cholesterol, sugar, sodium, and alcohol. Such a low-fat diet reduces your chances of getting certain diseases and helps you maintain a healthy weight.

The Food Guide Pyramid

The Pyramid (opposite) is an outline of what to eat each day. It's not a rigid prescription but a general guide that lets you choose a healthful diet that's right for you. By eating the suggested servings from each food group each day, you'll be enjoying a diet that not only gives you the nutrients you need, but at the same time, the right amount of calories to maintain or improve your weight. You'll also be following a diet that helps you keep your intake of fats and saturated fats low. This is important, because most American diets are too high in fat, especially saturated fat.

The five major food groups in the Pyramid (the three lower sections) are needed for good health. No one food group is more important than another — for good health you need them all! Each of the food groups provides some but not all of the nutrients you need. Foods in one food group cannot replace those in another.

How many calories do you need each day?

The Pyramid shows a range of servings for each major food group. The number of servings that are right for you depends on how many calories you need — based on your age, sex, size, and your lifestyle, that is, how active you are. Almost everyone should have at least the minimum number of servings listed for each group.

Here are three calorie level suggestions, based upon recommendations of the National Academy of Sciences and on calorie intakes reported in national food consumption surveys.

1,600 Calories— appropriate for many sedentary women and some older adults

2,200 Calories— appropriate for most children, teenage girls, active women, and many sedentary men (pregnant and breastfeeding women may need more calories)

2,800 Calories — appropriate for teenage boys, many active men, and some very active women

A day's sample diet

	1,600 Calories	2,200 Calories	2,800 Calories
Grain Group	6 servings	9 servings	11 servings
Vegetable Group	3 servings	4 servings	5 servings
Fruit Group	2 servings	3 servings	4 servings
Milk Group	2 to 3 servings*	2 to 3 servings*	2 to 3 servings*
Meat Group (ounces)	5 servings	6 servings	7 servings
Total Fat Grams	53	73	93
Total Added Sugars	6 teaspoons	12 teaspoons	18 teaspoons

* Women who are pregnant or breastfeeding, teenagers, and young adults to age 24 need 3 servings.

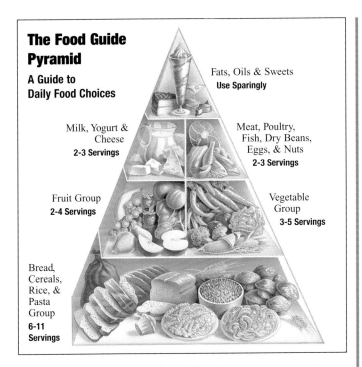

The Food Guide Pyramid
A Guide to Daily Food Choices

Fats, Oils & Sweets
Use Sparingly

Milk, Yogurt & Cheese
2-3 Servings

Meat, Poultry, Fish, Dry Beans, Eggs, & Nuts
2-3 Servings

Fruit Group
2-4 Servings

Vegetable Group
3-5 Servings

Bread, Cereals, Rice, & Pasta Group
6-11 Servings

The Food Groups

Breads, cereals, rice, and pasta — eat 6 to 11 servings a day

At the base of the Pyramid are foods from grains — breads, cereals, rice, and pasta. These foods provide complex carbohydrates, which are an important source of energy, especially in low-fat diets. They also provide vitamins, especially those from the B group, as well as many minerals and fiber. Choose foods made from whole grains whenever possible. They contain fiber that helps prevent constipation and helps keep our digestive system healthy. Eat foods in this group made with little fat or sugars more often, such as English muffins, bread, and pasta. Go ahead, enjoy croissants, cakes, cookies, and pastries — but not often, as they are high in both fats and sugars.

Vegetables — eat 3 to 5 servings each day

Nutrition experts agree: Vegetables are low in fat, are good sources of fiber, and are good for us. Many vegetables are rich in antioxidant nutrients, vitamin C, and beta-carotene (which the body converts to vitamin A). They also contain phytochemical compounds that have been linked to reducing the risk of certain diseases, such as heart disease and cancer. They are also low in fat and provide fiber.

Fruits — eat 2 to 4 servings each day

Fruits are fabulous — in flavor and nutrition. Both fruits and fruit juices provide important amounts of vitamins A and C, potassium, and fiber too. Choose from fresh fruits, fruit juices (without added sugar), frozen, canned (in juice, not heavy syrups), and dried fruits. Eat whole fruits often, as they are higher in fiber than fruit juices. Citrus fruits, some melons, kiwis, and berries are especially high in vitamin C, so eat them often for immunity and healing.

Meats, poultry, fish, dry beans, eggs, and nuts — eat 2 to 3 servings each day

These high-protein foods provide protein for growth and cell repair, the B vitamins that help metabolize energy, iron which is needed to carry oxygen in the blood, and zinc which is necessary for growth and repair. The total number of 2 to 3 servings from this group equals 5 to 7 ounces of cooked lean meat, poultry, or fish each day, or equivalents of cooked dry beans, eggs, peanut butter, or nuts.

Milk, yogurt, and cheese — eat 2 to 3 servings each day

Dairy foods such as milk, yogurt, and cheese are the best source of calcium, needed for strong bones and teeth and to help prevent osteoporosis. They also provide vitamins such as riboflavin (B_2) and minerals. To keep the calories and fat intakes low, choose low-fat or skim milk, plus products made from them. Go easy on high-fat cheese and ice cream; look for low-fat cheeses and reduced-fat milk desserts, such as frozen ice milk and yogurt.

Fats, oils, and sweets — use sparingly

The Dietary Guidelines recommend that Americans limit fats in their diets to 30 percent of calories from fats. Fat contains more than twice as many calories per gram as either carbohydrates or proteins.

What's a serving?

Breads, cereals, rice, and pasta

1 slice of bread	1 ounce of ready-to-eat cereal	½ cup of cooked cereal, rice, or pasta

Vegetables

1 cup of raw leafy vegetables	½ cup of other vegetables cooked or chopped raw	¾ cup of vegetable juice

Fruits

1 medium apple, banana, orange	½ cup of chopped cooked, or canned fruit	¾ cup of fruit juice

Milk, yogurt, and cheese

1 cup of milk or yogurt	1½ ounces of natural cheese	2 ounces of processed cheese

Meats, poultry, fish, dry beans, eggs, and nuts

2 to 3 ounces of cooked lean meat, poultry, or fish	½ cup of cooked dry beans or 1 egg counts as 1 ounce of lean mea 2 tablespoons of peanut butter or ⅓ cup of nuts counts as 1 ounce of lean meat

Recipe and Fruit Analyses

All recipes have been analyzed for their nutritional, vitamin, and mineral content, based upon the current USDA Nutrient Database for Standard Reference, using additional data from food manufacturers, where appropriate. The Daily Values, the standard values developed by the Food and Drug Administration (FDA) for use on food labels, were used to determine the following terms and symbols found throughout this book (see also pages 140 and 141):

✓✓✓	or excellent	at least 50% (half)
✓✓	or good	25% to 50% (one-quarter to one-half)
✓	or fair	10 to 25% (one-tenth to one-quarter)
Ⓥ	denotes that a recipe is suitable for vegetarians.	

Note: Recipes contribute other nutrients, but the analyses only include those that provide at least 10% of the Daily Value. Vitamins and minerals, when negligible, are not included.

Super Fruit

Delicious nutrition for health and good eating

WELCOME TO THE WONDERFUL WORLD OF FRUIT—a world
packed with vital vitamins, necessary minerals, essential
fiber, and, of course, flavor. Fruits play an important part
in keeping you healthy and feeling your best. Consider
the possibilities: frosty fruit drinks to start the day, fresh
sparkling salads, savory supper dishes, good-for-you side
dishes, and delicious desserts. And don't forget that fruits
are convenient snacks to eat "as is." Turn the pages and
find out how to choose the best fruits; how to slice, peel,
and pit them; how to freeze them,
then defrost them. Discover the
great taste that fruits impart to
dishes, any time of day, any
season of the year.

Fabulous fruits for a healthy diet

Whatever the season, fabulous fruits abound — from ripe fresh peaches, plums, and berries in the summertime to crisp apples in the fall, and juicy pears in the winter. At any time, frozen, dried, or canned fruits are readily accessible any time of year. With such bounty, it's easy to get two to four servings of fruits each day.

Why eat fruit?

The fabulous flavors of fruits are well known. But that's only one reason to eat fruits. Nutritionally, fruits are low in fat and sodium and are cholesterol free. Most fruits are full of vitamins and minerals — especially vitamin C in citrus fruits, melons, and strawberries; beta-carotene (for vitamin A) in yellow-orange fruits; potassium in bananas; and iron in dried peaches and prunes. Many dried fruits offer significant fiber.

An increasing number of studies show that people who eat a lot of fruits and vegetables are at less risk of developing heart disease, strokes, and certain cancers. Although the specific components still must be identified, antioxidant vitamins and minerals play an important role, possibly in conjunction with different fibers and natural plant chemicals.

▲ Best fruits for energy (top to bottom) – plantains, bananas, dried fruits (apples, figs, and apricots), and fresh dates.

▼ Best fruit for bioflavonoids (top to bottom) – cantaloupe, citrus fruits (oranges, limes, lemons), grapes, papaya, apricots, and cherries.

What nutrients can do

• Vitamins C and E and beta-carotene act as antioxidants, while the minerals of zinc, selenium, copper, and manganese are part of antioxidant enzyme systems in the body. They have the ability to delay or prevent oxidation, which produces highly damaging free radicals. Free-radical damage ages us and causes oxidative changes that increase the risk of heart disease and the growth of cells that can initiate cancers. Vitamin E prevents the oxidation of vitamin A, polyunsaturated fatty acids, and other fats. It also protects the lungs from pollutants and helps maintain healthy blood cells.

• Bioflavonoids are another type of antioxidant. They act as anti-inflammatory agents and work with vitamin C to boost immunity and strengthen blood capillaries.

super fruit

Best fruits for fiber (top to bottom) — banana, orange, apple, and dried fruits. ▶

Best fruits for vitamin C (top to bottom) — oranges, kiwi, strawberries, and black currants. ▼

▲ Best fruits for beta-carotene (top to bottom) — mango, cantaloupe, peach, papaya, and apricots.

◀ Best fruits for minerals (top to bottom) — bananas (potassium); apricots, particularly dried (iron); and prunes (potassium and iron).

super fruit

11

Reaching the Food Guide Pyramid target
2 to 4 servings of fruits each day

It's easy to enjoy 2 to 4 servings of fruits each day. For example:

Breakfast	either a glass of fruit juice or or a piece of fruit alone or sliced on cereal	= 1 serving
Lunch	a main-dish fruit salad or a piece of fruit for dessert	= 1 serving
Main meal	a fruit dessert, such as fruit pudding or a slice of fruit pie	= 1 serving
Snack	a piece of fruit	= 1 serving
Total		**= 4 servings**

• B vitamins are vital for healthy nerves and for releasing energy from food during digestion. Although in general, fruits are not as good a source of B vitamins as other foods, such as cereals, citrus fruits are an excellent source of folate, one of the B vitamins, also referred to as folic acid.

• Fiber comes in several varieties; many are found in fruits. Soluble fiber, such as the pectin in fruits that makes jams gel, helps lower levels of harmful blood cholesterol. Insoluble fiber, from the skin and fibrous structure of fruits and seeds, helps prevent constipation and associated digestive problems.

• Potassium works with sodium to maintain blood pressure. Most Western diets contain too little potassium and too much sodium, often from processed foods. Potassium-rich fruits like bananas and oranges are useful for getting the balance right.

Which are the best fruits to eat?

Eating a wide variety of fruits is best for you, as different fruits contain different nutrients. To spread your intake of different types of fruits, survey the fruit markets and discover new varieties. Choose from yellow-orange fruits (apricots, mangoes, melons, nectarines, peaches), citrus fruits, berries (blackberries, blueberries, black currants, raspberries, strawberries), exotic fruits (custard apples, dates, guavas, kiwis, litchis, passion fruits, papayas, pomegranates), and other favorites (apples, bananas, cherries, grapes, pears, pineapples, plums, watermelons).

To maximize the vitamin and mineral intake of fruits, choose fruits in season, whenever possible. Eat them raw, as even quick cooking reduces their nutrient content. Cooked, canned, and frozen fruits are still quite high in nutrients. In fact, frozen fruits contain more vitamins than tired fresh fruits. Fruits canned in fruit juice have less sugar than those canned in syrup, plus they have a more fruity flavor.

Are organic fruits better?

Many people feel that choosing organic fruits — that is, ones grown without artificial pesticides — is best, even though they are often more expensive. In reality, the hazards from possible pesticides on fruits are minimal. Government regulations strictly control the use of pesticides. The Environmental Protection Agency registers which pesticides may be used on food and sets upper limits for pesticide residues in individual foods. The Food and Drug Administration (FDA) monitors the levels of these pesticide residues in fruits yearly.

The golden rule: Before eating fruits, especially unpeeled ones, thoroughly wash them to remove some of the surface pesticides, waxes, and other treatments.

How can desserts be healthy?

Puddings based on fruit make a delicious nutritional ending to a meal. They do not need to be high in fat and sugar to be rich and sweet. A good example is a bread pudding made of bread and low-fat milk, then packed with dried fruits. All of these ingredients help meet the daily values for many nutrients.

Fruity bread pudding
Bread pudding provides fruit, carbohydrates (bread), protein (eggs), and dairy foods (milk).

Eating lots of different **fruits** is the best way to take advantage of the vital nutrients each contributes.

▲ Yellow-orange fruits (top to bottom), such as nectarines, apricots, and peaches, provide beta-carotene, as well as some B vitamins and vitamin C.

Berries of all kinds (top, clockwise), such as strawberries, blackberries, raspberries, gooseberries, blueberries, and red currants) give us vitamin C, plus fiber. ▶

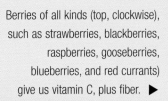

▲ Citrus fruits (top to bottom), such as grapefruits, limes, lemons, oranges, and kumquats, are packed with vitamin C and also provide fiber.

Other fruits (top to bottom) contribute vitamin C (pineapple), energy (pears), vitamin E and the antioxidant beta-carotene (plums), fiber (apples), and potassium (bananas). ▼

◀ Of the many and varied exotic fruits (top to bottom), fresh dates provide vitamin C, fiber, and lots of energy; kiwis are loaded with vitamin C, plus some potassium; guavas give vitamin C and fiber; passion fruits have vitamins A and C; and papaya offers vitamins A and C and fiber.

A new look at favorite fruits

Whatever the season, we can buy many of our favorite fruits at local supermarkets, greengrocers, and farm stands. Thanks to local growers and fruit importers, we often have our pick of such luscious and nutritious fruits as apples, bananas, berries, citrus fruits, pears, peaches, and a variety of melons. Enjoy them often!

An ABC of common fruits

While we think of citrus fruits as supplying mainly vitamin C, fruits also contain fair amounts of beta-carotene, which the body converts into vitamin A, plus some of the B vitamins and minerals such as iron, potassium, zinc, and copper. All the fruits here are low in calories and are fat free. Use the serving size to help count up to 4 fruits a day.

When buying and storing fruits, choose the freshest ones you can find. Buy in small quantities, which you know you will use up quickly. Choose fully ripe fruits if you're serving them the same or the next day. Remember, the vitamin content, especially vitamin C, varies according to freshness.

Apples (1 medium-size apple = 5 ounces)

It has long been said that "an apple a day keeps the doctor away." One study has shown that eating up to three apples a day for a month can help lower blood cholesterol levels. This is probably because apples contain soluble fiber (pectin) and an antioxidant called quercetin. So now we might add to the adage "… and 2 apples a day keeps the specialist away!"

◆ Choose firm, bright, crisp apples. Store in the refrigerator for up to 2 weeks; bring to room temperature before eating.

Apricots, peaches, and nectarines (3 apricots, 1 medium-size peach or 1 medium-size nectarine = 5 ounces)

Apricots are fair sources of the antioxidants of beta-carotene and vitamin C. An average serving of 3 apricots also provides a little potassium, copper, and dietary fiber. Peaches and nectarines share similar nutrition characteristics, with less vitamin C, beta-carotene, and fiber than apricots. The darker the color of the fruit, the higher the carotenoid content, so

white-flesh peaches and nectarines contain less beta-carotene.

◆ Choose firm plump fruits that give slightly when you feel them and have even-colored skins, with no brown spots. Do not buy fruit that is green near the stem end. It is unripe and will just go soft and mushy. To ripen fruits, take a brown paper bag, pierce it in several places, put the fruits inside, and store at room temperature for 1 or 2 days. Store ripe fruits in the refrigerator for up to one week.

Bananas (1 medium-size banana = 5 ounces)

Bananas contain high levels of natural sugars. They are a better source of energy than refined sugary foods, for they have a lot more to offer. Bananas really are a super fruit! One medium-size banana contains a fair amount of the daily value (DV) of vitamin C (17%DV) and 13%DV of potassium, which promotes proper metabolism and muscle function. It is a fair source of vitamin B_6 and provides a little folate (5%DV).

◆ If eating bananas immediately, choose yellow fruit with a few brown specks; otherwise select fruit with green ends. To ripen, store uncovered at room temperature; for faster ripening, store in a perforated paper bag at room temperature. Do not refrigerate bananas, as this turns the skins black.

Berries (1 cup berries = 3½ ounces)

The purple, dark red, and blue colors of many berries, such as black currants, blackberries, loganberries, raspberries, and strawberries, as well as dark cherries and black grapes, come from anthocyanin flavonoids, antioxidants that have been linked to reducing the risk of heart disease.

● Blackberries are an excellent source of vitamin C (50%DV) and of dietary fiber (35%DV).

● Black currants are outstandingly high in vitamin C, containing more than three times the DV in a serving. Black currants also contain fair amounts of potassium (18%DV) and fair amounts of fiber (19%DV).

apples

raspberries

bananas

nectarines, peaches,
and apricots

black currants
and blackberries

gooseberries

cranberries

strawberries

blueberries

- Blueberries are a good source of vitamin C (32%DV); they contain antioxidants and nutrients similar to cranberries.
- Cranberries are a good source of vitamin C (25%DV) and provide a fair amount of fiber. Drinking cranberry juice regularly can help prevent urinary tract infections such as cystitis. Cranberry juice contains a compound that prevents the most common bacteria, which cause the inflammation of the bladder wall, called cystitis.
- Gooseberries, which are only in season in the summertime, are an excellent source of vitamin C (69%DV) and a good source of dietary fiber.
- Raspberries, delicious any time, are an excellent source of vitamin C (51%DV) and a fair source of fiber (22%DV). Compared to strawberries, they contain less than half the amount of vitamin C but twice as much fiber.
- Strawberries are an excellent source of vitamin C (141%DV) — even ounce per ounce, slightly more than oranges. They also provide a little folate (7%DV).

◆ Choose brightly colored berries that are firm, juicy, and plump, with no white patches or mold. Select blueberries and blackberries with a white "bloom" and currants that are shiny. Avoid juice-soaked packages. Refrigerate berries in a single layer on a paper-towel lined plate (do not wash or cover). Use within 2 days. To serve, wash with cold water and pat dry.

Cherries (20 cherries = 3 ounces)

Sweet fresh cherries are great for snacking and provide a fair amount of both vitamin C (16%DV) and fiber (8%DV).

◆ Buy and store as berries (see left).

Citrus fruits (1 medium orange, ½ grapefruit, 20 kumquats)

All citrus fruits — such as oranges, grapefruits, lemons, limes, mandarins, clementines, satsumas, and kumquats — are very nutritious. They are an excellent source of vitamin C: one large orange provides 89%DV of vitamin C. The membrane that surrounds each juicy section is a common source of flavonoids and fiber. Pink grapefruits contain beta-carotene.

◆ Choose firm, well-shaped fruits that feel heavy for their size. Do not buy fruits with bruises or soft patches, and avoid fruits that have shriveled skins. Store citrus fruits in the refrigerator or at room temperature. The thick skin of citrus fruits helps to prevent them from drying out.

Grapes (1 cup = 3½ ounces)

Deliciously sweet, grapes provide 6% of the DV of vitamin B_1 (thiamine) and vitamin B_6, plus 5%DV of potassium. Red and black grapes have antioxidant properties, as they are high in bioflavonoids (passed into the wine made from these grapes).

◆ Choose plump grapes that are firmly attached to their stems, either shiny or with a bloom. Avoid grapes that are shriveled. Store grapes in the refrigerator for up to 5 days.

lemons, oranges, limes, and kumquats

cantaloupe

cherries

grapes

pears

plums: Ace, damsons, and greengages

rhubarb   watermelon

Melons (1 medium-size wedge = 8 ounces)

Whatever the season, you can usually find a selection of ripe melons in the market — cantaloupes, Crenshaws, honeydews, Persians, and Santa Claus (Christmas). All provide vitamin C; those with orange flesh contribute beta-carotene.

◆ Most melons are scented, but not all, so aromas are usually signs of ripe melons. Most ripe melons yield slightly to pressure at the stem end. Avoid buying melons if damaged or bruised. Store unripe melons at room temperature and ripe ones in the refrigerator for up to 1 week. After cutting melons, wrap in plastic wrap and refrigerate.

Pears (1 medium-size pear = 5 ounces)

Pears are slightly higher in calories than many other fruits, so they make great quick-energy snacks. Plus, they are one of the most easily digested fruits. One medium-size pear provides a fair source of fiber (19%DV) and vitamin C (11%DV), plus a little copper (9%DV) and a little potassium (6%DV).

◆ Choose firm pears that are fragrant, brightly and evenly colored, and slightly soft when you touch them. Avoid fruits with blemishes or soft spots. To ripen pears, store at room temperature; refrigerate ripe pears up to 3 days.

Plums (2 large red Ace plums = 6 ounces)

There are many varieties of plums, such as large red Ace plums, small oval indigo damsons, and small greengages.

One serving of plums (2 medium) provides a good source of vitamin C (31%DV) and a fair source of fiber (17%DV).

◆ Choose plums with good color, unshriveled skins, and free of brownish bruised spots. Select fruits that give slightly when touched and without any hint of fermentation. Ripen plums at room temperature, then refrigerate them for up to 2 days.

Rhubarb (6 tablespoons stewed rhubarb)

Actually a vegetable, rhubarb is often used like a fruit in cooking. It provides a little vitamin C and potassium (4%DV).

Watermelons (1 medium-size wedge = 8 ounces)

Perfect summertime treats, watermelons are comprised of more than 90% water, and great on a hot summer's day. One medium-size wedge is a good source of vitamin C (32%DV) and a fair source of vitamins B_6 (14%DV) and B_1 (11%DV).

◆ Buy and store as for melons (see left).

The vitamin C–iron connection

Fruits such as oranges, strawberries, and kiwis, which are rich in vitamin C, have been shown to improve the body's absorption of iron from vegetable sources. This fact is especially important for vegetarians and for the increasing number of people cutting down on red meat, which is the traditional source of iron in the diet.

super fruit

Fruits from around the world

Whatever the season, tropical and exotic fruits are now easy to find in specialty fruit markets and fruit stands. Many are becoming favorites to eat "as is," while others make wonderful contributions to salads, desserts, and sorbets, as well as nutritious complements to savory main dishes.

An ABC of tropical fruit

Exotic and tropical fruits brighten our fruit markets, often with signs telling us what they are, where they're grown, and how to use them. The unusual fruits featured here offer a nutritious combination of important vitamins and minerals, as well as bright colors and flavors that spark up dishes they appear in.

Yellow and orange fruits, such as mangoes, papayas, persimmons, carambolas (star fruits), and tamarillos, are particularly good sources of antioxidants such as beta-carotene and vitamin C. The fresh varieties have the best texture, a brighter color, and more flavor than cooked.

Asian pears (1 medium-size pear = 4 ounces)

Crunchy, amazingly juicy, and slightly sweet, Asian pears range from large and golden brown to small and pale yellow, with thin skins that may be sprinkled with russeting. Also known as apple pears, Oriental pears, Chinese pears, and *nashi* (Japanese for pear), Asian pears keep their shape, crispness and firmness, even after cooking. One medium-size pear is a fair source of fiber (16%DV) and a little vitamin C (8%DV).

◆ Unlike common pears, Asian pears are hard when ripe; they're in season from late summer to early fall. When stored in the refrigerator, Asian pears keep longer than apples. Enjoy them raw, peeled or unpeeled, and chilled, as well as cooked.

Cactus (prickly) pear (1 medium-size pear = 3½ ounces)

Pear-shaped and prickly like a cactus, prickly pears come from several varieties of cactus. Their skin colors vary from green to purplish red; their sweet brightly colored pulp, from light yellow-green to bright red. Prickly pears have an aroma like watermelon, and have many hard black seeds. The flesh is a fair source of vitamin C (24%DV) and magnesium (22%DV).

◆ Cactus pears are ripe when they give slightly when gently pressed, but do not feel soft or squishy. If fruits are firm, let them ripen at room temperature, then store them in the refrigerator for up to 1 week. Prickly pears are best when served cold. To serve, peel the pears, section them, lift out the fruit, and discard the seeds.

Cape gooseberries (1 cup gooseberries = 5 ounces)

Also called golden berries, ground cherries, and physalis, cape gooseberries, at first glance, look like Chinese lanterns, thanks to their papery skins. The ripe berries hiding inside are golden and opaque. Their piquant taste makes them perfect with meats; they're also great in jams and pies. One cup of berries provides a good source of vitamin C (26%DV) and a fair source of niacin (20%DV) and thiamine (10%DV).

◆ Choose yellow or orangy cape gooseberries (they're found from March to July). Spread them out, still in their papery husks, on an uncovered plate; refrigerate up to a month. Before serving, remove the berries from their skins.

Carambolas or star fruits (1 carambola = 4½ ounces)

Glossy, golden, fragrant, and juicy, these fruits resemble decorative stars when cut crosswise. They're delicious to eat "as is" (no peeling is needed) in salads, savory poultry dishes, or desserts. One star fruit is an excellent source of vitamin C (45%DV), plus a little copper (8%DV).

◆ Choose juicy-looking fruits with good color. If the fruits are green, let them ripen at room temperature until yellow. Store ripe fruits in the refrigerator for up to 2 weeks.

carambolas or star fruits

super fruit

Asian pears

custard apples

cactus pears or prickly pears

dates

cape gooseberries

feijoas

figs

guavas

Custard apples/cherimoyas (1 medium-size apple = 3½ ounces)

Looking like plump, yellowish-green pine cones with shiny black seeds, these custardy tropical fruits taste like pineapples, papayas, and bananas combined. One medium-size custard apple is a fair source of both vitamin C (20%DV) and riboflavin (10%DV), and provides a little potassium (8%DV).

◆ Choose custard apples that are heavy for their size and even in color, with no dark areas. Look for them from November through May. To ripen, store at room temperature; then refrigerate for up to 4 days. Serve custard apples well chilled. Halve them, remove seeds, and scoop out flesh with a spoon.

Dates (10 large dates = 3 ounces)

Native to the Middle East, the name comes from the Greek *daktulos*, meaning finger. Fresh dates are energy dynamos: these little fruits contain 55% sugar (23 calories per date).

◆ Choose plump, glossy fruits and store them in a plastic bag in the refrigerator, for up to 3 days. Look for fresh dates in specialty markets from late summer through mid-fall. To serve, just pit them and eat them (no peeling is needed).

Feijoas (1 medium-size feijoa = 1¾ ounces)

Egg-shaped fruits with thin skins, these cream-colored feijoas have the flavors of pineapples, lemons, and mint. One feijoa provides a fair source of vitamin C (11%DV) and a little folate (5%DV). When ripe, feijoas are delicious raw and cooked.

◆ Choose fruits that have rich perfume. Ripen them at room temperature a few days until soft. Peel, then slice and eat.

Figs (1 medium-size fig = 1¾ ounces)

Ranging in color from purple-black to almost white, figs have fragrant flesh with many tiny edible seeds. Great candied, too. One medium-size fig is a fair source of fiber (13%DV).

◆ Figs bruise easily, so are best bought before fully ripe, from June through October. To eat, just cut off the stem and enjoy.

Guavas (1 medium-size guava = 3 ounces)

Typically, guavas are small, oval fruits with thin skins from yellow-green to purple-black, flesh from off-white to bright red, and edible seeds. When ripe and fragrant, guavas have the flavors of pineapples and lemons. Great in jams, jellies, and sauces. One medium-size guava provides an excellent source of vitamin C (275%DV) and a fair source of fiber (10%DV).

◆ Slightly green guavas will ripen at room temperature; refrigerate and eat within 2 days. Peel, then slice and eat.

super fruit

19

Kiwis (1 medium-size kiwi = 2¾ ounces)

Brown and suede-like on the outside, kiwis are brilliant, beautiful, and green on the inside with tiny edible black seeds. Their flavor is sweet and tart, unique with hints of strawberry and pineapple. Peel and slice kiwis into salads and desserts, or use as a garnish. Just one medium-size kiwi provides an excellent source of vitamin C (124%DV) and a fair source of fiber (10%DV), a little potassium (7%DV) and folate (7%DV).

◆ When buying kiwis, choose firm fruits that yield only slightly to the touch. Kiwis continue to ripen after harvesting (they are picked while still hard). Ripen them at room temperature, then store in the refrigerator for up to 2 weeks.

Litchis/lychees (3 litchis = 1 ounce)

Also called Chinese plums, litchis have rough, bright red shells, soft white flesh and a delicate sweet perfumy flavor. Eating 3 raw litchis supplies 36% of the DV of vitamin C.

◆ Choose plum litchis that are plump, without any cracked or shriveled shells. The rosier they look, the fresher they are. Store litchis, still in their shells, in the refrigerator for up to 2 weeks, but expect them to lose a little of their perfume. Shell, seed, and eat "as is," or slice into salads or desserts.

Mangoes (1 medium-size mango = 7 ounces)

Large, luscious, juicy fruits with bright orange flesh, mangoes taste exotically sweet and slightly tart. One medium-size mango provides excellent sources of vitamin C (96%DV) and vitamin A (54% DV from beta-carotene). It is a fair source of fiber (19%DV), vitamin B_6 (14%DV), and copper (11%DV).

◆ Although many varieties exist, most mangoes have green skins that turn yellow, with bright red blushes. They are most plentiful from May to September, but imported ones are available year-round. Choose fruits that look plump, with a pleasant perfume (the stronger the scent, the riper the mango). Ripen mangoes inside a paper bag at room temperature. When mangoes are ripe, peel, pit, and eat right away; do not store.

Papayas (1 medium-size papaya = 5 ounces)

Often confused with dark-brown banana-looking fruits called pawpaws, papayas are vivid golden-skinned fruits with bright sunset-orange, juicy, silky flesh and shiny grayish black seeds. They have a sweet fragrance with a slightly exotic flavor. One medium-size papaya provides an excellent source of vitamin C (144%DV) and a fair source of beta-carotene (19%DV).

kiwis

pineapples

litchis/lychees

papayas

mangoes

passion fruits

rambutans

quinces

◆ Choose papayas that feel slightly soft when you touch them. To ripen green papayas, place in a closed paper bag at room temperature. When papayas are ripe, refrigerate and eat within 1 week. Simply peel, halve, scoop out seeds, slice, and enjoy.

Passion fruits (1 medium-size passion fruit = 5 ounces)

Although not nutritional champions, passion fruits do contribute some vitamins A and C, and if you don't strain out the edible seeds, they are a good source of fiber. Their major culinary contribution is their intense exotic fragrance. The granadilla is a close relative of the passion fruit.

◆ Choose fruits that are large and heavy. Passion fruits with dimpled skin are ready to use. If skins are smooth, ripen at room temperature for a few days until wrinkled. Store ripe fruits in the refrigerator for up to 1 week. Just peel and enjoy.

Persimmons (1 medium-size persimmon = 6 ounces)

Also known as sharon fruits and kaki fruits, persimmons vary in color and shape — from round and yellow with slightly pointed bases (Hachiyas or Japanese persimmons) to small, red-orange tomato shapes (Fuyus). One medium-size fruit supplies a good source of vitamin C (21%DV).

persimmons
(sharon fruits)

◆ Choose soft, plump persimmons, not mushy ones. Some varieties are bitter until they ripen; others, such as Fuyus, are tangy-sweet, even when firm. Buy from October to February. Ripen persimmons at room temperature; refrigerate for up to 3 days. Cut off stems (do not peel), slice, and eat, seeds and all.

Pineapples (1 cup pineapple chunks = 5½ ounces)

Native to Central and South America, pineapples resemble pinecones on the outside; golden, juicy, perfumy, and sweet on the inside. One cup of fresh chunks provides a good source of vitamin C (40%DV) and a fair source of thiamine (B$_1$).

◆ Pineapples will not ripen after picking (the starch will not convert to sugar), but keeping them at room temperature for a few days decreases the fruit's acidity and makes them taste sweeter. Choose ripe pineapples that feel slightly soft with a sweet aroma near the stem end. To serve, cut off the spiny top, peel, cut out the eyes, slice crosswise, remove core, and eat!

pomegranates

Pomegranates (1 medium-size = 5½ ounces)

Large orange-colored fruits, pomegranates have many edible crunchy seeds that look like glistening red jewels. One medium-size fruit offers a fair source of vitamin C (16%DV).

◆ Choose fruits that are heavy for their size. Cut the fruit in half, peel, break into sections, discard the cream-colored membrane, and eat only the seeds. Buy pomegranates in the fall; they keep well in the refrigerator for up to 2 months.

Quinces (1 medium-size quince = 3¼ ounces)

These yellowish fruits with creamy flesh look and taste like crosses between apples and pears. One medium-size quince provides a fair amount of vitamin C (23%DV); but because quinces need to be cooked to become edible, most of this vitamin is lost. One quince also provides a little fiber (7%DV), known as pectin, making it ideal for jellies and preserves.

◆ Choose fruits that are aromatic. Store ripe quinces in a plastic bag in the refrigerator for up to 2 months. Wrap each fruit individually, as quinces bruise easily. Peel before using.

Rambutans (1 medium-size rambutan = 3½ ounces)

Known as "hairy litchis" because their flesh is like that of litchis, rambutans contain half the vitamin C of litchis.

◆ Choose plump fruits that soften when ripe. Discard shells.

Tamarillos (1 medium-size tamarillo = 2 ounces)

Known as "tree-tomatoes," these egg-shaped fruits have smooth, glossy skins. Depending on variety, tamarillos can be deep-red, purple, or yellow with a red, yellow, or dark apricot-colored flesh that resemble pleasantly tart tomatoes. To benefit from their good amounts of vitamin C, eat raw in a salad.

◆ Choose firm, heavy fruits. Ripen tamarillos at room temperature until slightly soft and fragrant. Store in the refrigerator for up to 1 week. Peel by parboiling for a minute, then pull off skins.

tamarillos

Concentrated fruity goodness

Dried fruits prove that great things come in small packages. They are a powerhouse of goodness, especially in flavor and nutrients. And being small, compact, and portable, they make terrific snacks for all, especially children.

dried Hunza apricots

An ABC of dried fruit

Drying fruits is an old, traditional method of preserving them. Reducing the moisture content and concentrating sugars means that bacteria cannot thrive. Whether fruits are dried in the sun or by industrial processes, the results are the same. Ounce per ounce, dried fruits have more carbohydrates (sugars) and calories than fresh fruits. This makes dried fruits a great energy snack, especially for children. However, weight watchers should eat them sparingly.

Many dried fruits are good sources of minerals, such as iron, potassium, and copper. The drying process has an adverse effect on some water-soluble vitamins, especially vitamin C. Other water-soluble B vitamins, such as riboflavin and niacin, are less affected by the drying process and are retained in the dried fruits.

Since dried fruits are concentrated in flavor, they give both a flavor boost and an energy boost to any dish they appear in.
- Dried apples: 1 cup provides 32%DV for fiber and 10%DV for potassium.
- Dried apricots: They are a powerhouse of nutrients, including iron, a mineral that is lacking in many women's diets and essential in the prevention of anemia. One cup provides an excellent source of beta-carotene (62%DV), which the body converts into vitamin A, and for potassium (51%DV). It is also a good source of dietary fiber (40%DV), iron (34%DV), and copper (27%DV).
- Dried bananas: 1 cup has almost four times the calories of fresh and are a good source of potassium (43%DV).
- Dried blueberries: 1 cup provides 36%DV for fiber.
- Dried cherries: They are lower in sugars than many other dried fruits. One cup of dried cherries gives 30%DV for beta-carotene (vitamin A) and a small amount of iron (6%DV).
- Dried cranberries: 1 cup dried cranberries is a fair source for fiber (24%DV), which is a little less fiber than raisins. They are sweetened when dried.
- Dried currants: 1 cup is a good source for fiber (39%DV), potassium (37%DV), copper (34%DV), and iron (26%DV).
- Dried dates: 1 cup provides an excellent source of fiber (62%DV). It also provides a good source of potassium (34%DV) and copper (25%DV), plus a fair source of niacin (20%DV) and vitamin B_6 (18%DV).
- Dried figs: These are best known as an excellent source of fiber. One cup provides 67% of the daily value for fiber. It is also an excellent source of potassium (40%DV), as well as a good source of copper (32%DV), magnesium (30%DV), calcium (28%DV) and iron (24%DV).
- Dried mangoes: Provide a useful amount of dietary fiber.
- Dried papayas: Retain some of their brilliant color when dried. They are a useful source of fiber.
- Dried peaches: Known as an excellent source of fiber (56%DV), peaches are also a good source of potassium (45%DV), iron (37%DV), and niacin (35%DV). Dried peaches are a fair source of beta-carotene, which provides 22% of the DV for vitamin A.
- Dried pears: 1 cup dried pears provides an excellent source of fiber (56%DV), a good source of copper (34%DV) and potassium (27%DV), plus a fair source of iron (22%DV).
- Dried pineapples: These dried fruits are a good source of fiber, but have less beta-carotene (for vitamin A) than fresh pineapples.

dried strawberries

super fruit

- Prunes: Well known for their laxative effect, 1 cup of dried prunes provides 46% of the DV of fiber; just 3 prunes offer 10% of the DV for fiber. Also, 1 cup supplies a good source of copper (37%DV) and potassium (36%DV).
- Raisins and sultanas: 1 cup provides a good source of potassium (35%DV) and copper (25%DV). They are also a fair source of iron (20%DV).

Sweet snacks

Most of the carbohydrates in dried fruits are in the form of sugars, but unlike refined sugar, these foods are a valuable source of fiber and nutrients, making them a good snack food. They are also excellent to use in cooking. When combined with fresh fruits, they can help reduce sugar or replace it.

Fruit and fiber – the GI factor

GI stands for Glycemic Index, which is a ranking of foods based on their effect on blood-sugar levels. Low-GI foods break down slowly, releasing energy gradually into the bloodstream, resulting in a smaller rise of blood sugar. High-GI foods break down more quickly and cause a larger rise of blood sugar. Low-GI foods are better for you, because they can help control hunger, appetite, and weight, as well as lower the raised blood fats. Fruits with a low GI include cherries, grapefruits, apples, bananas, grapes, kiwis, mangoes, peaches, pears, plums, and dried apricots. Fruits with an intermediate GI include cantaloupes, papayas, raisins, and pineapples. Watermelon has a high GI.

Additives in dried fruits

Many dried fruits are treated with sulfur-based preservatives to prevent discoloration, as well as preserve and enhance the orange color of fruits, such as apricots and peaches. If dried fruits are unsulfured they are a less attractive brown color, plus they do not have the sharp tang of sulfured fruits. Potassium-based preservatives are used to prevent fungal and bacterial spoilage, particularly in ready-to-eat dried fruits that are partially hydrated for convenience. Fully dried fruits contain fewer additives. Dried fruits may also be coated with vegetable oil to make them glossy and prevent them from sticking and clumping.

Average calorie counts in ⅓ cup of dried fruits

dried apples = 70 calories

dried apricots = 102 calories

dried bananas = 113 calories

dried blueberries = 120 calories

dried sour cherries = 140 calories

dried cranberries = 130 calories

dried currants = 135 calories

dried dates = 162 calories

dried figs = 167 calories

dried mangoes = 150 calories

dried papayas = 140 calories

dried peaches = 126 calories

dried pears = 156 calories

dried pineapple = 140 calories

dried prunes = 127 calories

dried raisins = 144 calories

super fruit

Preparing and cooking fruits

Buy the best, freshest, ripest fruits you can find. If they need a little more ripening, store them at room temperature until they are ready to eat, then chill or serve. When ripe, most fruits have a perfumy fragrance and feel slightly soft. To preserve the nutrients in fruits, prepare them using minimal processing or cooking.

Golden rules for preparing fruit
- Wash fruits well to remove surface dirt, bacteria, and some surface pesticides. Rinse fruits well in cold water, then drain or dry.
- Avoid soaking fruits in water.
- Refrigerate berries, uncovered, on a plate lined with paper towels; wash berries just before serving.
- Peel fruits only when necessary, as vitamins and minerals are just below the skin. Fruit skins are a good source of fiber.
- Slice or dice fruits carefully with a serrated fruit knife.
- When slicing apples, bananas, nectarines, and peaches, sprinkle them with fresh lemon juice, as quickly as possible, to prevent them from browning and discoloring.
- If not cooking or eating immediately, cover prepared fruits with plastic wrap and store in the refrigerator.

- Prepare fruits as close to serving or cooking as possible.
- Whether poaching, boiling, stewing, or microwaving fruits, cook them for the shortest time possible. Use as little water or other liquid as you need.
- Avoid warming or reheating fruits a long time.

Saving vitamins and minerals
Vitamin A and the provitamin A precursor of beta-carotene are stable during mild heating, but are destroyed at higher temperatures. Vitamin E is destroyed gradually by heat; the higher the temperature and the longer the cooking time, the greater the loss. Vitamin C is the least stable vitamin, as it is vulnerable to heat, light, and oxygen. Plus it is water soluble and seeps into the cooking water, as do some minerals in fruits. So when cooking fruits, use the cooking water in the dish, or in sauces for fruit salads and desserts.

Good partners for fruit desserts

Cream on top – your choice
Topping fresh berries or fruit puddings with cream is a delicious indulgence. You can choose just how much you'd like to indulge by taking a look at the chart below — the heavier the cream, the higher the fat and calorie content. Depending on which cream you choose, the flavor changes slightly, but they all make delicious accompaniments to fruits and fruit desserts. To help you choose the various options, here's how the calories and fat differ in 1 tablespoon of various creams:

Heavy whipping cream	51 calories	5.5 grams of fat
Sour cream	31 calories	3 grams of fat
Light cream	29 calories	3 grams of fat
Half & half	20 calories	2 grams of fat
Fat-free sour cream	9 calories	0 grams of fat

Yogurt – a better choice?
Yogurt is made by culturing (fermenting) milk with "friendly" bacteria to thicken it. Plain yogurt makes a good alternative to cream. But, like cream, yogurts differ in the amounts of calories and fat in 1 tablespoon:

Whole-milk yogurt	9 calories	0.5 grams of fat
Low-fat plain yogurt	9 calories	0.22 grams of fat
Nonfat plain yogurt	8 calories	0 grams of fat

Frozen yogurt is a delicious lower-fat substitute for ice cream. But it does contain a lot of sugar, and thus is high in calories.

The best of both
Whip a little heavy cream until stiff, then stir in the same amount of plain low-fat yogurt or fat-free sour cream. Add a little confectioners' sugar and flavor with a splash of pure vanilla extract and a dash of cinnamon.

Fruit coulis

Basically, coulis are very simple fruit purées, made with raw or cooked fruits, then sweetened if necessary. Coulis made with raw fruits retain more of the vitamin C content, which is reduced through even the briefest cooking. Almost any soft fruit can be used for an uncooked coulis — such as peaches, blackberries, gooseberries, and raspberries, to name just a few.

Berry coulis (uncooked)

Makes about 1 cup

½ pint fresh raspberries (1 cup)

¾ pint ripe strawberries, sliced (1 cup)

1 tablespoon fresh lemon juice

1 tablespoon confectioners' sugar, or to taste

2 tablespoons kirsch (cherry liqueur) (optional)

Preparation time: 15 minutes

1 In a bowl, mash the berries with a fork. Mix in the lemon juice and sugar, plus the kirsch, if you wish. Or, purée all of the ingredients in a food processor or blender until smooth.

2 Using a rubber spatula, push the mixture through a strainer into a small bowl. Chill the coulis before serving.

Blackberry coulis (cooked)

Makes about 1 cup

1 pint fresh blackberries (2 cups)

3 tablespoons sugar

2 tablespoons currant jelly

1 tablespoon fresh lemon juice

2 tablespoons crème de cassis (optional)

Preparation time: 15 minutes
Cooking time: 8 minutes

1 In a medium-size, heavy saucepan, place the blackberries, sugar, and jelly. Cook over low heat, stirring frequently, for 8 minutes or until the sugar dissolves and the fruit is soft and juicy. Taste and add more sugar if necessary.

2 Using a rubber spatula, push the mixture through a strainer into a small bowl. Stir in the lemon juice, plus the crème de cassis, if you wish.

Some more ideas

• Gooseberry coulis: For the coulis, combine 1 pint (2 cups) fresh gooseberries (blossom and stems removed), ¼ cup sugar, and 1 tablespoon of water in the saucepan (step 1) and cook as directed. Flavor with 2 tablespoons orange flower water or Cointreau (orange liqueur) (step 2).

• Blueberry coulis: Use 1 pint fresh blueberries, ¼ cup sugar, 2 tablespoons orange juice (step 1), and cook as directed. Stir in the lemon juice and crème de cassis (step 2).

• Quick coulis (uncooked): Purée 2 cups dry-packed frozen peaches or raspberries; proceed as in uncooked berry coulis.

Fresh mango and banana with berry coulis (above); Persian almond crème with currant coulis (right; see recipe, page 137).

A Great Start

Smoothies, muffins, and other breakfast treats

START THE DAY WITH LUSCIOUS FRUITS. Wake up to a tall icy glass of fresh citrus juices. Whirl up a smoothie from yogurt and fresh berries or a fresh fruit fizz from a mango, a peach, a couple of ripe apricots. Sip a banana shake made with milk and frozen yogurt, or whip up a refreshing icy slush from ripe strawberries and chunks of fresh pineapple. Bake a batch of yummy apricot-pecan muffins one morning, then make some banana-nut or fresh blueberry-walnut muffins the next. Spoon some dried berries over granola for a  treat that's low in fat but high in nutrition and flavor. Whatever your pleasure, you're on your way to eating 2 to 4 fruits a day.

Strawberry yogurt smoothie

Summertime is fresh strawberry time, and the perfect time for this flavorful drink. Whirl up the berries with yogurt and fresh orange juice to create this creamy refreshing "smoothie" that's high in vitamin C. It's a fast and healthy breakfast shake or a delicious low-calorie snack-in-a-glass, any time of the day.

Makes 4 smoothies

1 quart ripe strawberries, hulled (4 cups)
⅔ cup plain low-fat yogurt
½ cup fresh orange juice (1 large orange)
1 tablespoon sugar, or to taste

To decorate (optional)

4 small strawberries with leaves
4 thin round slices of unpeeled orange

Preparation time: 10 minutes

1 Rinse and drain the strawberries and place them in a food processor or blender. Add the yogurt, orange juice, and 1 tablespoon sugar. Process on the highest speed for about 15 seconds or until a well-blended purée forms, stopping to scrape down the sides of the container once or twice. Taste the mixture and sweeten with a little more sugar, if you wish.

2 For the smoothest of smoothies, strain the mixture, using a wooden spoon to push the drink through. Discard the strawberry seeds.

3 Pour into 4 tall glasses and serve immediately. If you wish to decorate the drinks, slit the strawberries and the orange slices halfway through the centers. Attach one berry and one orange slice to the rim of each glass.

More ideas

• Banana-berry smoothie: Add 1 small banana, cut into quarters (step 1). Because bananas tend to thicken drinks, increase the orange juice to ¾ cup. Taste the smoothie before adding the tablespoon of sugar (you may not need it).
• Fresh apricot-berry smoothie: For the fruits, use 2 cups peeled apricot slices and only 1 pint (2 cups) hulled ripe strawberries (step 1).

Healthy tips

• Strawberries are not only naturally sweet and delicious, but they are also an excellent source of vitamin C. Ounce per ounce, strawberries provide more vitamin C than fresh oranges. Vitamin C is an antioxidant that helps protect against cancer, may slow the aging process, and helps maintain the immune system.
• However you eat it, yogurt is good for you. It's high in calcium and phosphorus. Plus, it contains active bacterial cultures that "eat" the milk sugar (lactose), making yogurt a great dairy product for those people who have a milk intolerance.
• For your health's sake, choose low-fat plain yogurt, which is lower in calories than those yogurts sweetened with fruit purées.

Each smoothie (8 ounces) provides Ⓥ
calories 95, total fat 1g, saturated fat 0g, cholesterol 2mg, sodium 28mg, total carbohydrate 20g, dietary fiber 3g, protein 3g

✓✓✓ C
✓ B₂, folate, potassium, fiber

a great start

Mango, peach, and apricot fizz

Pick only perfectly ripe golden fruits for this drink — half a mango, a peach, and two apricots. Quickly purée them in a blender with a bottle of icy cold ginger ale, tonic, or sparkling mineral water. Use a freshly opened bottle, so you're sure to have plenty of fizz. Then serve immediately, while there are still plenty of bubbles.

Makes 4 drinks

½ large ripe mango (about 5 ounces)

1 large ripe peach (5 ounces)

2 large ripe apricots (3 ounces each)

1 liter ice-cold ginger ale (about 4 cups)

Crushed ice

To decorate (optional)

Fresh mint or lemon balm leaves

Preparation time: 10 minutes

1 Peel the mango. Cut the fruit away from the pit in large chunks and place in a blender or food processor.

2 Cover the peach and apricots with boiling water and let them stand for about 30 seconds, then drain and cool the fruits under cold running water. Slip off the skins and discard the pits. Cut each fruit into quarters and place them in the blender.

3 Pour enough ginger ale over the fruit just to cover. Process the fruit mixture on high for 15 seconds or until the mixture is completely smooth.

4 With the blender still running, pour in the remaining ginger ale through the opening in the cover. Process again until light and fizzy.

5 Half-fill 4 tall glasses with crushed ice and pour in the drink. Decorate each drink with fresh mint or lemon balm leaves, if you wish. Serve the fizzes immediately with wide straws or swizzle sticks.

More ideas

● Raspberry fruit fizz: For the fruit, use 1 cup fresh raspberries, 1 cup fresh cantaloupe chunks, and 1 large peeled, pitted peach (5 ounces). Substitute chilled plain seltzer for the ginger ale.

● Orange-berry fizz: For the fruit, use 2 cups fresh orange sections and 1 pint (2 cups) hulled fresh strawberries. Substitute icy cold sparkling mineral water for the ginger ale.

● For lighter drinks with more fizz: Add 6 ounces (¾ cup) more of the fizzy ingredient, such as ginger ale, seltzer, or sparkling water.

● For the calorie conscious: Use sugar-free ginger ale to reduce the calories.

Healthy tip

● These golden fruits whip up into a drink that's not only refreshing and fresh-tasting, but also very good for you. They provide a feast of vitamins. Mangoes, peaches, and apricots are full of beta-carotene, which the body converts into vitamin A. This is the vitamin that is essential for good vision and helps prevent night blindness. It is also believed to help prevent lung cancer.

Each drink (8 ounces) provides Ⓥ

calories 147, total fat 0g, saturated fat 0g, cholesterol 0mg, sodium 19mg, total carbohydrate 37g, dietary fiber 2g, protein 1g

✓✓ A, C

a great start

31

Banana and mango shake

Here's a great-tasting fruity milk shake that takes only five minutes to whirl up in a blender. It's so creamy, thick, and nourishing that it's the perfect breakfast drink to start the day. Delectable as a dessert, too.

Makes 2 shakes

½ large ripe mango (5 ounces)

½ small ripe banana (3 ounces)

⅔ cup low-fat milk (2% milkfat)

⅔ cup fresh orange juice

2 teaspoons fresh lime juice

1 teaspoon sugar

¼ cup frozen vanilla yogurt

To decorate (optional)

Sprigs of fresh lemon balm or mint

Preparation time: 10 minutes

1 Peel the mango and cut the flesh away from the pit in large chunks. Place the mango in a blender with the banana cut in half.

2 Pour in the milk, orange juice, and lime juice. Add the sugar and the frozen yogurt. Blend the shake on the highest speed for about 30 seconds or until the mixture is smooth and frothy.

3 Pour the shake into 2 tall glasses. Top each shake with a sprig of lemon balm or mint, if you wish. Best when served immediately.

More ideas

• Banana and peach shake: Substitute a large ripe, peeled, pitted peach for the mango half.

• Banana-berry shake: Substitute 1 pint (2 cups) hulled fresh strawberries for the mango half.

• Skimmed-down shakes: Use skim milk instead of 2% low-fat milk. Skim milk weighs in at only 85 calories per cup, compared to 120 calories for low-fat milk with 2% milkfat. Plus, skim milk has no fat, but it does have similar amounts of vitamins and minerals as the higher-fat milks.

• For the lactose-intolerant: If you cannot eat dairy products because they contain milk sugar (lactose), make this milk shake with 1 cup of soya milk, instead of the cow's milk, and omit the frozen yogurt.

Healthy tips

• Milk is an excellent source of calcium, protein, and phosphorus, which all help to build healthy bones and teeth. A diet rich in calcium also helps prevent osteoporosis.

• Bananas are an excellent source of potassium, which helps regulate the balance of fluids in the body.

• Mangoes are rich in vitamin C, as well as beta-carotene, which the body converts into vitamin A. These are both antioxidants that protect the body against damage by free radicals. Mangoes are also low in calories and high in fiber.

Each shake (12 ounces) provides Ⓥ

calories 201, total fat 3g, saturated fat 2g, cholesterol 7mg, sodium 59mg, total carbohydrate 41g, dietary fiber 3g, protein 5g

✓✓✓	C
✓✓	A
✓	B_1, B_2, B_6, folate, calcium, magnesium, potassium, fiber

a great start

Citrus wake-up

Instead of plain orange juice some morning, whisk up this frosty blend of citrus fruits. Begin with sweet juicy oranges; be sure to pick ones that feel heavy for their size, as this usually means they are filled with juice. Add a pink grapefruit, lime, and lemon, plus some shreds of fresh mint. It's a great way to start the day!

Makes 4 drinks

1 large lime

4 large juice oranges (see varieties at right; 1½ pounds)

1 medium pink grapefruit (about 12 ounces)

1 large lemon

¼ cup cold water

2 tablespoons sugar

2 tablespoons finely shredded fresh mint leaves

To decorate (optional)

4 thin round slices unpeeled lemon

4 thin round slices unpeeled lime

Preparation time: 15 minutes

1 Using a citrus zester or peeler, remove the zest from the lime; set aside ½ teaspoon.

2 Cut the lime, oranges, grapefruit, and lemon in half crosswise. Juice the fruits by using either an electric juicer or a citrus squeezer, preferably one that strains out seeds while allowing a generous quantity of pulp. If you don't have a squeezer, poke a fork into the flesh several times, then squeeze the juice from the fruit by hand, prodding with the fork now and again.

3 In a large pitcher, stir the citrus juices with the reserved lime zest, the water, sugar, and shreds of mint. Pour the drink into 4 glasses over a few ice cubes. Decorate the drinks, if you wish, with the slices of lemon and lime.

More ideas

• Look for oranges that are bright in color with no mold or spongy spots. Good choices include:

— Hamlins, usually from Florida, are perfect for juicing, because they are full of sweet juice and pulp, plus they are seedless.

— Imported Jaffa oranges, grown in Israel and other sunny regions, are sweet and fragrant, with a balance of tartness. Jaffa oranges are easy to spot at the market because of their vibrant, bright orange color.

— Valencias, one of the easiest oranges to find in the U.S., have a smooth, thin, deep orange skin, few seeds, and a sweet and golden juice.

• Mexican fruit gazpacho: Omit the lime and grapefruit; increase the lemons to 2. Juice only 2 of the oranges; peel and section the remaining 2. Cut up 1 small pineapple (3 cups fruit); peel and thinly slice 1 kiwi (½ cup slices). Mix and serve as a chunky fruit gazpacho or whirl it all up in a blender or food processor until it is frothy. Decorate with fresh mint leaves, if you wish.

• Summery sparkler: For a nonalcoholic summery drink, add 6 ounces (¾ cup) chilled lime- or lemon-flavored seltzer to the juicy mixture in the pitcher, just before pouring into the glasses (step 3).

Healthy tips

• Naturally, citrus fruits are one of the best sources of vitamin C. Being an antioxidant, vitamin C protects against cell damage by free radicals, which are produced in the body when oxygen is burned.

• Oranges and their juice contain a B vitamin called folate that is important for women of child-bearing age because it helps prevent birth defects.

Each drink (8 ounces) provides ⓥ

calories 144, total fat 0g, saturated fat 0g, cholesterol 0mg, sodium 2mg, total carbohydrate 39g, dietary fiber 6g, protein 3g

✓✓✓ C

✓ B_1, folate, calcium, potassium, copper, fiber

Frozen pineapple and berry slush

It looks like a frozen drink, it eats like a sorbet, and it tastes like a fresh fruit treat. This frozen fruit slush is quick to whip up in the morning. Try it as an afternoon snack or spoon it into sherbet glasses and serve as dessert. Keep a selection of chopped fresh fruit in your freezer, so you can make it anytime.

Makes 4 slushes

1 pint ripe strawberries, hulled (2 cups)
2 cups fresh pineapple chunks
1 cup ice cubes (about 8 large)
½ cup pineapple juice
2 tablespoons sugar, or to taste

To decorate (optional)
Sprigs of fresh pineapple mint

Preparation time: 20 minutes
Freezing time: at least 1½ hours for
   freezing fruit

Each slush (8 ounces) provides Ⓥ
calories 102, total fat 1g, saturated fat 0g,
cholesterol 0mg, sodium 2mg, total
carbohydrate 25g, dietary fiber 2g, protein 1g

✓   C

1 Freeze the fresh fruits. Put the ice cubes in a food processor or heavy-duty blender and pulse until they are finely crushed. Or, drop the ice cubes into a plastic bag and close; smash them with a rolling pin, then finish crushing them in a food processor or blender.

2 Add the frozen strawberries and pineapple chunks, the pineapple juice, and sugar. Pulse on high just until blended, but not liquified. Small pieces of fruit and ice should still remain.

3 Taste and add a little more sugar if you wish. Process a few seconds more just until blended, not liquified.

4 Spoon the slush into 4 tall glasses and decorate each with a sprig of pineapple mint, if you wish. Serve with long spoons.

More ideas

• Three-berry slush: Substitute ½ pint (1 cup) fresh blueberries and ½ pint (1 cup) fresh raspberries for the pineapple. Use ½ cup cranberry juice instead of the pineapple juice.

• Rosy peach slush: Instead of the fresh fruits, use 3 cups frozen dry-pack peach slices and 1 cup frozen dry-pack raspberries (both are available in your supermarket's frozen food section). Omit the pineapple juice and use only ¼ cup cranberry juice instead (step 2).

• Tropical slush: Substitute the strawberries and pineapple with 2 cups chopped, peeled mangoes and 2 cups cantaloupe chunks. Instead of pineapple juice, use orange juice (step 2).

• Slush-in-an-instant: When you have slush left over, freeze it in divided ice cube trays. Later, to quickly make a slush, just whip the cubes in a food processor or blender. If it's too thick, add a little extra fruit juice.

Healthy tips

• Both fresh and frozen pineapple contain a substance called bromelain, a digestive enzyme that can break down proteins. There is some evidence to suggest that bromelain may help to break up blood clots and may therefore be helpful in protecting against heart disease. Bromelain also has an anti-inflammatory action and has been used in the treatment of arthritis.

• A wide variety of fruit is now available frozen. These are convenient to have on hand and may be a better source of vitamins than some "fresh" fruits that may have been poorly stored, badly handled, or kept too long on the shelf. They are particularly useful for these slushes, where the texture of the fruit is not important.

• For a drink that's also high in vitamins A and C, try the Tropical Slush, using mango and cantaloupe (see "more ideas," left).

Apricot-pecan muffins

Any time can be muffin time, especially when you bake up these fresh apricot-pecan muffins. They come out of the oven light, moist, and cinnamony, with an extra helping of wheat bran for flavor and nutrition. If apricots are not in season, mix up the muffins with other fresh fruits, such as blueberries, strawberries, or bananas.

Makes 12 large muffins

2¼ cups all-purpose flour

1 cup packed light brown sugar

3 tablespoons wheat bran

1 tablespoon baking powder

1 teaspoon ground cinnamon

½ teaspoon grated lemon zest

¼ teaspoon salt

2 large eggs

6 tablespoons (¾ stick) unsalted butter, melted and cooled

1 cup low-fat milk (2% milkfat)

8 ounces ripe but firm apricots (about 5), peeled, pitted, and coarsely chopped (1 cup)

½ cup chopped pecans

Preparation time: 25 minutes

Baking time: 20 minutes

Each muffin provides Ⓥ

calories 264, total fat 10g, saturated fat 4g, cholesterol 52mg, sodium 78mg, total carbohydrate 40g, dietary fiber 1g, protein 5g

✓ A, B₁, B₂, iron

1 Preheat the oven to 375°F. Set out a muffin tin with 12 regular muffin cups, which measure about 2½" across the top and 1" deep. Butter the cups well or line with paper liners.

2 In a large bowl, mix the flour, sugar, wheat bran, baking powder, cinnamon, lemon zest, and salt. Make a well in the center and set aside.

3 In a large measuring cup, whisk the eggs until frothy and light yellow. Beat in the butter, then the milk, until well blended. Pour this mixture all at once into the well in the center of the flour mixture. Stir just until the dry ingredients are moistened, leaving some small lumps of the flour mixture in the batter. Do not overmix the batter, as this can make the muffins tough. With a rubber spatula, gently fold in the apricots and pecans.

4 Spoon the batter into the prepared muffin tin, filling the cups three-fourths full. Bake the muffins for 20 minutes or until the muffins are peaked and golden brown. The muffins are done when a wooden pick inserted in the center comes out almost clean, with a few moist crumbs clinging to it. Let the muffins cool in the tins for 3 minutes before removing them. These muffins are best when served piping hot or within a few hours of baking.

Healthy tips

• Health experts regularly recommend increasing the amount of fiber in our diet. These muffins help to do just that, especially when made with 1 cup of chopped dried apricots instead of fresh ones. They contribute both soluble and insoluble fiber, which is good for digestion, and also helpful in controlling the fat and sugar in the blood.

• Wheat bran is the indigestible outer fibrous part of the wheat grain. It is one of the richest sources of dietary fiber that helps keep the digestive system healthy.

More ideas

• Banana-nut muffins: Use ⅔ cup mashed ripe banana instead of the apricots (step 3).

• Fresh blueberry-nut muffins: Substitute 1 teaspoon grated orange zest for the lemon zest (step 2). Substitute 1 pint (2 cups) fresh blueberries for the apricots and ½ cup chopped walnuts for the pecans (step 3).

• Fresh strawberry muffins: Substitute 2 cups coarsely chopped, hulled ripe strawberries (buy 1 quart of berries) for the apricots (step 3).

• Fresh peach muffins: Use 2 cups coarsely chopped, peeled, ripe peaches (1 pound) instead of the apricots (step 3).

• High-fiber muffins: For the flour, use 2 cups all-purpose flour and ¼ cup whole-wheat flour (step 2).

Orchard spread

Save the fat calories by using this rich, lightly spiced purée of fresh and dried fruit instead of butter on warm toast or muffins. The recipe makes 4 cups, far more than is needed at one breakfast, but the spread keeps well in a covered jar in the refrigerator. Another day, try it for lunch in a sandwich with Cheddar cheese.

Makes 1 quart (4 cups)

1 pound tart cooking apples, such as Jonathan, McIntosh, Rome Beauty, peeled, cored, and coarsely chopped (3 cups)

1½ cups ready-to-eat dried pears (9 ounces)

1½ cups ready-to-eat dried peaches (9 ounces)

1½ cups apple juice

1½ cups water

½ teaspoon ground allspice

1½ teaspoons fresh lemon juice, or to taste

Preparation time: 30 minutes
Cooking time: 35 minutes
Cooling time: at least 1 hour

2 tablespoons of spread provide
calories 54, total fat 0g, saturated fat 0g, cholesterol 0mg, sodium 2mg, total carbohydrate 14g, dietary fiber 2g, protein 0g

1 In a large heavy saucepan, place the apples, pears, peaches, apple juice, water, and allspice. Bring the fruit mixture to a boil over high heat, stirring occasionally.

2 Reduce the heat to low and simmer, uncovered, for 30 minutes or until the mixture is reduced to a pulp and no liquid is visible on the surface. Stir frequently to prevent the mixture from sticking to the bottom of the pan.

3 Remove the pan from the heat and let the mixture cool slightly. Stir in the lemon juice, then taste and add a little more if the mixture is too sweet.

4 Transfer the fruit mixture to a food processor or blender and process until a thick purée forms. Let the spread cool at room temperature for about 1 hour before serving. The spread can be kept in a covered jar, refrigerated, for up to a week.

More ideas

• Just before serving, stir in some finely chopped blanched almonds. Tip: Add nuts just to the portion of the spread you are serving, as the nuts will soften if stored for more than a few hours.

• Mixed fruit spread: Substitute the dried pears and peaches with 3 cups (18 ounces) dried mixed fruits, such as blueberries, cranberries, pineapple, and golden raisins. Substitute 1½ cups fresh orange juice for the apple juice and ½ teaspoon ground ginger for the allspice.

• Vanilla peach spread: Increase the dried peaches to 3 cups (18 ounces) and omit the dried pears. Substitute 1½ cups fresh orange juice for the apple juice. Replace the allspice with a vanilla bean, discarding it after cooking (step 3) and before adding the lemon juice.

• Orange cranberry spread: Replace the dried peaches and pears with 3 cups (18 ounces) dried cranberries and substitute 1½ cups cranberry juice for the apple juice. Add 2 teaspoons finely grated orange zest with the allspice (step 1).

Healthy tips

• Apples are a good source of soluble fiber called pectin, which helps lower blood cholesterol levels. Soluble fiber absorbs large amounts of water from the intestinal tract, helping to prevent constipation.

• Dried peaches are a good source of vitamin A, iron, and potassium. Plus, they contain carotenes which protect against some cancers.

• Both dried peaches and dried pears are good sources of fiber.

• The sweetness of fresh fruit is concentrated in their dried forms, so a spread such as this one does not need additional sugar.

Spicy date, apple, and cheese dip

Their natural sweetness makes dates an excellent ingredient for desserts, cakes, and chutneys. Here, they are cooked until thick and smooth with an apple and aromatic spices, then blended with cream cheese to make a sweet and spicy dip for fresh fruits and vegetables. It also makes a great spread for toast, scones, and muffins.

Makes 1¼ cups

3 green cardamom pods or ½ teaspoon ground cardamom

1 extra-large cooking apple, such as Jonathan, McIntosh, Rome Beauty, peeled, cored, and coarsely chopped (1½ cups)

⅓ cup chopped fresh or dried dates

½ teaspoon ground cinnamon

⅛ teaspoon ground ginger

¾ cup water

8 ounces reduced-fat cream cheese (Neufchâtel), at room temperature

To serve

As a dip for crudités such as:

wedges of red and green apples; carrot, celery, and cucumber sticks; wedges of fresh pineapple; seedless grapes; ripe strawberries

Preparation time: 30 minutes
Cooking time: 15 minutes
Cooling time: at least 1 hour

2 tablespoons of dip provide Ⓥ

calories 92, total fat 4g, saturated fat 2g, cholesterol 8mg, sodium 129mg, total carbohydrate 13g, dietary fiber 1g, protein 3g

✓ A

1 If using cardamom pods, lightly crush them with the flat side of a chef's knife to split them open, then remove the seeds. Discard the pods and crush the seeds with the side of the knife. (This can be done with a pestle and mortar.) Or, use ground cardamom.

2 Mix the apple, dates, crushed cardamom seeds, cinnamon, and ginger in a medium-size saucepan, then pour in the water. Bring the mixture to a boil over medium heat, stirring occasionally.

3 Reduce the heat to low and simmer, uncovered, for 10 minutes or until the apple is tender and the dates are pulpy. Stir occasionally to prevent the mixture from sticking to the bottom of the pan. Remove the mixture from the heat to cool.

4 When the apple mixture is cool, stir the cheese in a medium-size bowl until creamy, then blend in the fruit mixture. Cover and refrigerate until serving time. (The dip will keep in the refrigerator for up to 3 days.)

5 Serve the dip in a shallow bowl or dish, place on a platter, and surround with an assortment of fruit and vegetable crudités.

Healthy tips

● Neufchâtel is cream cheese that is made with one-third less fat and is slightly more moist than regular cream cheese. It's perfect for adding creaminess and flavor to this dip. However, this reduced-fat cheese is not recommended by most manufacturers for use in baking.

● The apple and dried dates are high in fiber. Dates are an excellent source of potassium, which helps to regulate the balance of fluids in the body.

● Fiber can reduce blood cholesterol and help maintain a healthy digestive tract.

● Both cinnamon and cardamom are spices that help relieve indigestion.

More ideas

● Use this cream cheese dip as a filling between layers of spice cake.

● Try this dip as a filling for crêpes or as an accompaniment for French toast.

● Date, apple, and orange salsa: Omit the cheese (step 4) and stir in ½ cup chopped toasted almonds and 1 teaspoon grated orange zest instead. Serve with slices of lean roasted pork or grilled chicken.

a great start

Blueberry and cranberry granola

Start with a box of toasted low-fat raisin granola made from a crunchy blend of oats and wheat. Then toss in nuts, dried berries, sesame seeds, and sunflower seeds. Stir in maple syrup and orange juice for a little extra sweetness and flavor. Top with yogurt or milk for breakfast, or eat "as is" for a healthy snack.

Makes 6 cups

4 cups low-fat packaged raisin granola

½ cup dried cranberries (1¾ ounces)

⅓ cup dried blueberries (1¾ ounces)

¼ cup slivered blanched almonds

2 tablespoons light brown sugar

2 tablespoons sunflower seeds

1 tablespoon sesame seeds

2 tablespoons fresh orange juice

2 tablespoons maple syrup

2 tablespoons sunflower oil

Preparation time: 15 minutes

Baking time: 25 minutes

1 Preheat the oven to 325°F and set out a shallow baking pan with sides, about 10"x 15"x 1". In a large bowl, combine the granola, dried cranberries and blueberries, the almonds, sugar, and the sunflower and sesame seeds. Toss until well mixed.

2 Whisk the orange juice, maple syrup, and oil in a measuring cup. Drizzle this mixture slowly over the dry ingredients, tossing to make sure that the mixture coats everything lightly.

3 Spread out the granola mixture in a single layer in the pan. Bake for 25 minutes or until the mixture is slightly crisp and lightly browned. Stir the mixture every 10 minutes to ensure even browning.

4 Remove the granola from the oven and let cool. Store in an airtight container at room temperature for up to 2 weeks. Serve with low-fat vanilla yogurt or milk.

Healthy tips

● This is a delicious way to get plenty of fiber, B vitamins, and essential fatty acids.

● Oats are particularly high in soluble fiber, which can help lower blood cholesterol levels, thus possibly reducing the chance of heart attacks.

● The sunflower seeds add a unique flavor. Among the seeds, they are one of the richest in niacin, iron, and potassium.

● Nuts and seeds are one of the best sources of vitamin E, which is the nutrient needed to make red blood cells and build muscle tissue.

More ideas

● Golden granola: Replace the cranberries and blueberries with ½ cup chopped dried apricots, ½ cup golden raisins, and ½ cup flaked coconut (step 1).

● Cherry-berry granola: Substitute ½ cup dried cherries for the cranberries (step 1).

● Four-fruit granola: For the fruit use: ⅓ cup *each* dried blueberries, dried cherries, dried cranberries, and dark raisins (step 1).

● Honey-nut granola: Substitute ¼ cup chopped hazelnuts for the almonds (step 1). Substitute 3 tablespoons honey for the maple syrup (step 2).

Each serving (½ cup) provides Ⓥ

calories 210, **total fat** 6g, **saturated fat** 0g, **cholesterol** 0mg, **sodium** 40mg, **total carbohydrate** 38g, **dietary fiber** 3g, **protein** 4g

✓✓	B_1, B_2, niacin, B_6, B_{12}, folate, E, zinc
✓	A, D, E, iron, magnesium, fiber

a great start

Raw Vitality

Fruit and vegetable salads, so good for you

EATING FRESH FRUITS RAW, WITHOUT COOKING, lets you enjoy not only the nutrients they offer but also their fabulous fresh flavors. In the summertime, slice up some fresh berries for that extra helping of vitamin C, and sweeten with a sprinkling of sugar. Serve a fresh salad in a cantaloupe shell, or toss watermelon chunks with bites of feta cheese and slices of fresh nectarines. Turn a fresh spinach and citrus salad into a main dish with shreds of prosciutto, and spice up tropical fruits with bits of red chili pepper. Add crispy radicchio to a creamy apple and green grape salad. You'll soon discover the wonders of fruit salads, both savory and sweet.

Berry salad with passion fruit

Tart, sweet, and juicy, berries come in many varieties — from bright and delicate raspberries to sweet strawberries, from plump little blueberries to rich fragrant blackberries. Thanks to importers, you can buy almost all berries in any season. If one kind is not available, substitute another. Passion fruits add a tart edge.

Makes 6 servings

1 quart ripe strawberries, hulled and cut in half (4 cups)

½ pint fresh red raspberries (1 cup)

½ pint fresh blackberries (1 cup)

¾ cup fresh blueberries

½ cup mixed fresh red currants and black currants, removed from their stalks

2 passion fruits

3 tablespoons sugar, or to taste

1 tablespoon fresh lime or lemon juice

Preparation time: 10 minutes

1 In a large serving bowl, combine the strawberries, raspberries, blackberries, blueberries, red currants and black currants in a bowl.

2 Cut each passion fruit in half. Holding a strainer over the bowl of berries, spoon the passion fruits and seeds into the strainer. Rub the flesh and seeds briskly to press all the juice through the strainer onto the berries. Reserve a few of the seeds left in the strainer and discard the rest.

3 Add the sugar and lime juice to the berries. Gently toss. Sprinkle over the reserved passion fruit seeds. Serve immediately or cover and chill briefly.

More ideas

• Instead of passion fruits, add 3 tablespoons crème de cassis. Chill until ready to serve.

• Berry salad with fresh peach sauce: Omit the passion fruits. Peel, pit, and purée 2 large ripe peaches. Sweeten with 3 tablespoons sugar, 1 tablespoon fresh lemon juice and ½ teaspoon pure vanilla extract. Lace with 1 tablespoon peach brandy, if you wish.

• Fresh berry sundae: Scoop frozen vanilla yogurt into dessert plates and spoon the berries over the top. Sprinkle with a few toasted almonds, if you wish.

Healthy tips

• Vitamin C countdown: Comparing the same weight of each fruit, fresh black currants weigh out on top in vitamin C. One 3½ ounce (½ cup) serving of black currants contributes 180mg of vitamin C, as compared to fresh strawberries with 56mg, fresh raspberries with 25mg, and fresh blackberries with 21mg. Vitamin C is still recognized as essential in strengthening the blood vessels and providing a basis for strong bones and teeth. This vitamin is also known for helping to maintain the immune system. Because vitamin C is an antioxidant, it may also prevent the damaging processes that can lead to heart disease and cancer.

• This feast of summer fruits is particularly healthful. It's rich in dietary fiber and vitamin C. The passion fruits add vitamin A, which is essential for healthy skin and good vision; they also contain beta-carotene, which is an important antioxidant.

Each serving provides Ⓥ

calories 100, total fat 1g, saturated fat 0g, cholesterol 0mg, sodium 4mg, total carbohydrate 24g, dietary fiber 6g, protein 1g

✓✓✓	C
✓	fiber

raw vitality

48

Pimm's melon cup

The classic Pimm's cup is the original gin-sling drink, believed to have been created more than a century ago in London's financial district. Today, England bottles and exports it as Pimm's No. 1, a slightly sweet liqueur, flavored with herbs, spices, and fruit extracts. Here, it's tossed with fresh fruits for a summery dessert.

Makes 4 servings

1 small cantaloupe (about 1 pound)

1 small honeydew or Crenshaw melon (about 1 pound)

1 pint ripe strawberries, hulled and sliced (1½ cups)

1 large pear (6 ounces), cut into ½-inch chunks

½ small cucumber, diced (½ cup)

2 star fruits, sliced ¼ inch thick

3 ounces Pimm's liqueur (6 tablespoons)

2 tablespoons shredded fresh mint

To decorate (optional)

Edible flowers, such as blue borage, pansies, or rose petals

Preparation time: 25 minutes
Marinating time: 20 minutes

Each serving provides   Ⓥ

calories 218, **total fat** 1g, **saturated fat** 0g, **cholesterol** 0mg, **sodium** 39mg, **total carbohydrate** 45g, **dietary fiber** 6g, **protein** 3g

✓✓✓	C
✓✓	A, potassium
✓	B₁, niacin, B₆, copper, fiber

1 Cut both melons in half crosswise and scoop out the seeds from the center. Using a melon baller or a small spoon, scoop out balls of melon into a large bowl. With a tablespoon, scoop out any remaining melon into the bowl, leaving smooth shells.

2 Add the strawberries, pear chunks, and diced cucumber to the melon in the bowl. Set aside 4 star fruit slices for decoration. Dice the remaining slices and add to the bowl.

3 Drizzle the Pimm's over the fruit, sprinkle with the mint, and toss gently to mix well. Cover with plastic wrap and let macerate in the refrigerator for 20 minutes.

4 Pile the fruit mixture into the shells and decorate with the reserved slices of star fruit and edible flowers, if you wish.

More ideas

• Nonalcoholic fruit basket: For the Pimm's, substitute a mixture of 3 tablespoons fresh orange juice and 3 tablespoons honey (step 3).

• Luncheon salad: For the fruits and vegetables, use 1 small honeydew or Crenshaw melon, 1½ cups sliced, hulled strawberries, 1 large crisp red apple such as Delicious or Cortland, 1 cup seedless green grapes, 2 peeled sliced kiwis, and ½ cup diced cucumber. Omit the cantaloupe, pear, star fruits, and Pimm's. In a large bowl, toss 6 cups mesclun salad leaves, 2 cups watercress, and ½ cup chopped green onions. Arrange on 4 salad plates and spoon the fruit on top. Add a scoop of low-fat cottage cheese and sprinkle with the shredded fresh mint and ½ cup chopped pistachios.

• Edible flowers: Unless you have a blooming flower garden, look for edible flowers at a gourmet market or fruit stand. Depending on the season, you'll find blue borage blossoms (an herb plant with a cucumber flavor), nasturtiums, pansies, rose petals, squash blossoms, and even violets.

Healthy tips

• This delicious combination of fresh fruits provides a healthy serving of fiber and vitamins, especially vitamin C. The orange-fleshed melon contributes beta-carotene, which the body converts into vitamin A, an important antioxidant.

• The latest research studies show that during pregnancy, women should avoid alcohol altogether. But for the general population, a small amount of red wine is now believed to reduce detrimental blood cholesterol and prevent blood clot formation. Both are associated with lowering the risk of heart disease.

raw vitality

Apple and date salad

Here's a sweet-fruit combination of apples, dates, and grapes, with the surprise crunch of red pepper and the bitter bite of radicchio. It's all topped with a creamy yogurt-based dressing and toasted hazelnuts. Enjoy it for lunch with chunks of crusty bread, or serve it as a side dish for dinner with smoked turkey or grilled chicken.

Makes 6 side- or 4 main-dish servings

Yogurt dressing

¾ cup plain low-fat yogurt

¼ cup reduced-fat mayonnaise

1 tablespoon fresh lemon juice

1 teaspoon sugar

¼ teaspoon salt

¼ teaspoon white pepper

Salad

¼ cup chopped hazelnuts (2 ounces)

1 pound unpeeled green apples, such as
 Granny Smith, cored and cut into
 ½ inch dice (3 cups)

1¼ cups fresh or dried dates, pitted and
 coarsely chopped

1 cup seedless green grapes

1 medium-size red sweet bell pepper, seeded
 and chopped (1 cup)

1 cup thinly sliced celery

24 radicchio leaves (2 large heads)

2 tablespoons chopped fresh parsley

Preparation time: 20 minutes

Each serving provides ⓥ

calories 275, **total fat** 10g, **saturated fat** 1g, **cholesterol** 5mg, **sodium** 148mg, **total carbohydrate** 50g, **dietary fiber** 7g, **protein** 4g

✓✓	C, E, fiber
✓	B$_1$, B$_6$, magnesium, potassium, copper

1 First, make the dressing. Whisk the yogurt, mayonnaise, lemon juice, sugar, salt, and pepper in a large bowl until well blended.

2 In a small dry frying pan, stir the hazelnuts over moderate heat until they look toasted and you can smell the nutty fragrance. Set aside to cool.

3 Add the apples to the bowl with the dressing and toss until the pieces are well coated. Stir in the dates, grapes, red pepper, and celery.

4 Break off the bottom third of the radicchio leaves and add to the salad. Pile the salad on a large plate or in a shallow serving dish and arrange the tops of the radicchio leaves around the edge. Sprinkle the toasted hazelnuts and parsley over all.

More ideas

● Either fresh or dried dates work well in this salad. Look for fresh dates in specialty fruit markets from late-summer through mid-fall. Dried dates are available year-round, pitted or unpitted, in packages or in bulk.

● Vinaigrette dressing: Substitute the yogurt dressing with this vinaigrette. In a medium-size measuring cup, whisk 6 tablespoons olive oil, 2 tablespoons red wine vinegar, ½ teaspoon Dijon mustard, ½ teaspoon sugar, plus salt and pepper to taste. Toss with the salad.

Healthy tips

● This recipe provides plenty of dietary fiber from apples with their skins, celery, radicchio, and, of course, dates. Fiber is essential to keep the digestive tract healthy.

● Dates contain natural sugars; in fact, 60% to 70% of their weight comes from natural sugars. When these sugars come wrapped in fiber, as in dates, the body can control a steady release of glucose into the bloodstream. Dates are also a good source of potassium, niacin, and pyridoxine.

● Bacteria (*Streptococcus thermophilus* and *Lactobacillus bulgaricus*) are traditionally used to make yogurt. Recent research indicates these bacteria can be helpful in maintaining the balance between the "friendly" and "unfriendly" bacteria that live in the digestive tract. They do so by producing lactic acid, which inhibits the growth of the unfriendly bacteria that can cause illnesses.

Watermelon and feta salad

Here's a summery cheese salad, created with a nod toward the Mediterranean. The salty tang of creamy feta cheese contrasts with the sweet watermelon and juicy golden nectarines. A mix of arugula, endive, and leaf lettuce adds a slightly peppery taste, while the toasted seeds give a nice crunch. With bread, you have lunch!

Makes 6 side-dish or 4 main-dish servings

Lemon dressing

3 tablespoons extra virgin olive oil

2 tablespoons fresh lemon juice

¼ teaspoon salt

¼ teaspoon freshly ground black pepper

Salad

½ small watermelon (1 pound)

2 large nectarines or peaches (1 pound)

6 ounces mixed salad greens, including arugula, endive, and leaf lettuce (6 cups)

8 ounces feta cheese, crumbled (2 cups)

3 tablespoons toasted pumpkin seeds or sunflower seeds

Preparation time: 20 minutes

1 First, make the dressing. Put the oil, lemon juice, salt, and pepper into a pint-size jar with a screw top. Cover and shake until well blended.

2 Using a serrated knife, cut the watermelon into bite-size chunks, discarding the rind and all of the seeds. Toss into a large salad bowl.

3 Cut the nectarines in half (do not peel) and pit them. Place the nectarines on a cutting board, cut-side down, and cut lengthwise into thin slices; toss with the watermelon chunks. Tear the salad greens into bite-size pieces and add to the fruit. Toss to mix.

4 Crumble the feta cheese over the salad. Sprinkle the seeds over the top; serve. Tip: To serve the salad later, prepare the salad through step 2, cover with plastic wrap, and refrigerate. Proceed with steps 3 and 4 right before serving.

More ideas

• Pear and Gorgonzola salad: Instead of the watermelon and nectarines, use 1 pound ripe, cored, thinly sliced red Bartlett or Comice pears, and 1 quart sliced ripe strawberries (3 cups). Use 8 ounces creamy Gorgonzola cheese instead of the feta cheese. Include radicchio in the mix of salad leaves.

• Try using toasted walnuts in place of the toasted pumpkin or sunflower seeds.

Healthy tips

• The golden nectarines and peaches contain the antioxidant beta-carotene, which the body converts into vitamin A. Watermelon contains a fair amount of vitamin C.

• In addition to protein, the cheese provides calcium. Feta cheese is high in sodium (salt), actually more than twice as much as found in the same quantity of Cheddar. To reduce the salt, soak the feta in milk for 30 minutes. Then rinse the cheese in a strainer under running water and pat dry on paper towels.

• Toasted pumpkin and sunflower seeds contain a variety of useful minerals, including phosphorus, magnesium, and copper, as well as fiber and protein. Both types of seeds are rich sources of fat, but mostly the more healthful unsaturated type.

• Sunflower seeds are one of the best sources of vitamin E, which helps to maintain red blood cells and muscle tissue.

Each side-dish serving provides Ⓥ

calories 249, total fat 18g, saturated fat 7g, cholesterol 33mg, sodium 519mg, total carbohydrate 17g, dietary fiber 2g, protein 8g

✓✓	C
✓	A, B$_1$, B$_2$, B$_6$, B$_{12}$, folate, calcium, magnesium, potassium, zinc

raw vitality

Tropical fruit with coriander

Once considered exotic and hard to find, mangoes and kiwis are now plentiful and popular. Here, they're tossed with crunchy cucumber and red onion, then spiced with red chili and fresh lime dressing. Surprisingly delicious!

Makes 4 servings

Chili and coriander dressing

3 tablespoons sunflower oil

3 tablespoons fresh lime juice

1 tablespoon golden honey

2 tablespoons chopped fresh coriander

¼ teaspoon salt

¼ teaspoon freshly ground black pepper

1 fresh red chili, seeded and minced

Tropical fruit salad

2 large red onions

1 large mango, ripe but firm

2 large kiwis

½ small cucumber

Preparation time: 30 minutes

Marinating time: 30 minutes

Each serving provides ⓥ

calories 229, total fat 11g, saturated fat 1g, cholesterol 0mg, sodium 142mg, total carbohydrate 34g, dietary fiber 5g, protein 3g

✓✓✓	C
✓	A, B$_6$, folate, magnesium, potassium, copper, fiber

1 First, make the dressing. Put the oil, lime juice, honey, coriander, salt, pepper, and chili into a pint-size jar with a screw top. Cover and shake until well blended.

2 To make the salad, peel the onions and cut in half lengthwise. Place each half on a cutting board, cut-side down, and cut crosswise into thin semicircles. Separate into half-rings (you need 1½ cups of onions) and spread in a large shallow dish. Drizzle with the dressing, cover with plastic wrap, and marinate at room temperature for 30 minutes.

3 Cut the mango in half lengthwise, cutting down each side of the pit, then carefully lift the fruit away from the pit. Peel off the skin and place the mango halves on a cutting board, cut-side down. Using a serrated fruit knife, cut lengthwise into thin slices. Combine the mango slices, onions, and any remaining liquid in a salad bowl.

4 Peel the kiwis and slice crosswise into thin slices, ⅛ inch thick; add to the salad bowl. Cut the cucumber in half lengthwise (do not peel), and place on the cutting board, cut-side down. Cut crosswise into semicircles and add to the salad bowl. Drizzle with the dressing and toss gently.

Healthy tips

• Kiwis are excellent sources of vitamin C. Ounce per ounce, they each contain more vitamin C than an orange. In fact, one kiwi provides almost 100% of the recommended daily value of vitamin C. Mangoes are exceptionally high in beta-carotene, which the body converts into vitamin A. Both fruits are good sources of potassium, which helps maintain proper balance of fluids in the body.

• Ounce per ounce, chilies are also richer in vitamin C than citrus fruit. However, to get this benefit, you would have to eat more chilies than you probably want.

More ideas

• Minted tropical fruit salad: Substitute 3 tablespoons slivered fresh mint leaves for the coriander (step 1).

• Fruit market salad: Use 2 large navel oranges instead of the mango (step 3). Peel the oranges, removing all the white pith. Using a serrated fruit knife, cut the fruits into segments between the membranes and lift out the sections. Squeeze all the juice from the membranes and add to the salad. Cut 2 large ripe plums in half (do not peel), slice ¼ inch thick, and add to the salad bowl with the kiwi and cucumber slices (step 4).

raw vitality

56

Citrus and spinach salad

Spinach salads are traditional favorites, and this one comes with several taste-surprises. There's chunks of sweet melon, fragrant and juicy oranges, and colorful ruby-red grapefruit. The best surprise of all is the thinly sliced prosciutto, full of spice, cured to perfection, and imported from the Parma province in Italy.

Makes 6 side-dish servings

Balsamic dressing

3 tablespoons balsamic vinegar

3 tablespoons extra virgin olive oil

3 tablespoons light cream

2 teaspoons golden honey

¼ teaspoon salt

¼ teaspoon freshly ground black pepper

Citrus and spinach salad

3 large navel oranges

2 extra-large ruby-red grapefruits

8 ounces baby spinach leaves, well washed
(about 6 cups)

1 small cantaloupe, peeled and cut into bite-
size chunks (2 cups, about 1 pound melon)

4 green onions, white parts only, very thinly
sliced (½ cup)

6 ounces thinly sliced prosciutto (Parma ham)
cut into shreds (1 cup)

Preparation time: 30 minutes

Each side-dish serving provides

calories 246, total fat 10g, saturated fat 2g,
cholesterol 21mg, sodium 529mg, total
carbohydrate 31g, dietary fiber 6g, protein 11g

✓✓✓	C, A
✓✓	B₁, folate, potassium
✓	B₂, niacin, B₆, calcium, iron, magnesium, copper, fiber

1 First, make the dressing. Put the vinegar, oil, cream, honey, salt, and pepper into a pint-size jar with a screw top. Cover and shake until well blended.

2 To make the salad, use a citrus zester or peeler to remove fine shreds of zest from one orange. Set aside. Working over a medium-size bowl to catch any of the juices, peel the 3 oranges, then the grapefruits, using a serrated fruit knife; be sure to remove all of the white pith.

3 Cut between the membranes of the fruits, lift out the fruit sections, and place in the bowl with the juices.

4 Add 2 tablespoons of the combined grapefruit and orange juices to the dressing and shake again to blend. Taste and add more citrus juice, salt, and pepper, if you wish.

5 Place the spinach in a large serving bowl. Add the orange and grapefruit sections and any juices in the bowl, the cantaloupe, and green onions. Toss to evenly distribute the ingredients among the spinach leaves. Shake the dressing once more, then pour it over the salad and toss again. Scatter the shredded prosciutto over the top of the salad and sprinkle on the orange zest. Serve the salad immediately, as it can wilt quickly if it's allowed to stand.

Healthy tips

• This salad is an excellent source of vitamin C, thanks to all of the fruits as well as the spinach. Because cooking and cutting foods destroys vitamin C, it is best to leave the spinach leaves whole and to serve the salad as soon after tossing as possible.

• Cantaloupe contains the antioxidant beta-carotene, which is converted into vitamin A by the body.

More ideas

• Zesty spinach salad: To add a peppery flavor to this salad, use only 6 ounces spinach leaves (4 cups); add 2 ounces watercress leaves (2 cups). Tear off the watercress leaves from their stalks; use only the leaves, discarding the stems. Watercress is an excellent source of vitamin C, as well as beta-carotene.

• Citrus, spinach, and gorgonzola salad: Make a vegetarian salad by omitting the prosciutto. Substitute 6 ounces of bite-size chunks of creamy, savory, rich gorgonzola cheese for the prosciutto.

• Dressing with a difference: In place of the balsamic vinegar, use 3 tablespoons raspberry, apple cider, or white wine vinegar in the dressing.

raw vitality

Savory Ways with Fruit

Main dishes with unexpected fruit surprises

IT'S SUPPERTIME — AND THAT MEANS MORE CHANCES TO SERVE FRUITS. Simmer up delicious surprises of sweet, spicy, and savory dishes with fresh and dried fruits. Team up shrimp with fresh pineapple and pomegranate seeds... chicken with fresh apricots and cumin... or grilled pork chops with Asian pears and star anise. Try stewing lamb chunks with figs, stir-frying mangoes with steak, or roasting root vegetables with dried fruits. By adding fruits to supper dishes, you add nutrition and flavor too.

Thai shrimp and pineapple

Pretend you're in Malaysia enjoying a seaside supper of fresh seafood. This recipe has all of the typical tastes and flavor surprises: jumbo shrimp, fresh pineapple, cream of coconut, and hot Thai spices. An authentic treat!

Makes 4 servings

2 large yellow onions, peeled and quartered

2 large garlic cloves, peeled

2 tablespoons sunflower oil

1 large fresh red chili, cut in half, seeded, and thinly sliced

2 teaspoons ground coriander

1 teaspoon ground cumin

1 teaspoon turmeric

1 teaspoon white pepper

2 cups low-sodium chicken broth or bottled clam juice

¼ cup canned cream of coconut

2 tablespoons Thai fish sauce or soy sauce

2 tablespoons light brown sugar

1¼ pounds uncooked jumbo shrimp

½ medium-size fresh pineapple (about 12 ounces), peeled, cored, and cut into bite-size chunks (2 cups)

3 green onions, cut into 1½-inch lengths, then shredded (about ⅓ cup)

Seeds of 1 pomegranate, for garnish

Preparation time: 45 minutes

Cooking time: 24 minutes

Each serving provides

calories 381, **total fat 13g, saturated fat 4g, cholesterol 131mg, sodium 614mg, total carbohydrate 46g, dietary fiber 3g, protein 21g**

✓✓✓ C

✓ B_1, niacin, B_6, B_{12}, calcium, iron, magnesium, potassium, copper, fiber

1 In a food processor, place the onions and peeled garlic cloves, then pulse until finely chopped. Or, mince by hand.

2 In a large nonstick skillet, heat the oil over medium-high heat. Add the onion-garlic mixture and sauté for 7 minutes or until soft and golden.

3 Add the chili and all of the spices to the pan and stir to mix with the onions. Pour in the chicken broth and add the cream of coconut, fish sauce, and sugar. Bring the mixture to a simmer, reduce the heat to medium-low, cover, and simmer gently for 10 minutes.

4 Meanwhile, peel the shrimp, leaving the last tail section on each one, if you like. Using a shrimp peeler or the tip of a small sharp knife, devein the shrimp, removing both the vein on the curved top side and the one underneath in the belly of the shrimp.

5 Stir the shrimp into the sauce and cook very gently, uncovered, for about 4 minutes or until they turn pink. Watch carefully and do not overcook, as the shrimp may toughen.

6 Stir in the pineapple and green onions. Cook just 2 minutes more to warm the pineapple through. Sprinkle with the pomegranate seeds and serve.

Healthy tips

• Shrimp are an excellent source of vitamin B_{12}, which is needed for making red blood cells. They are also a good source of selenium, an important antioxidant that works with vitamin E to protect the body against free radicals and promote normal body growth and fertility.

• Throughout history, onions and garlic have been credited as cure-alls. And for good reason: Recent research suggests that adenosine in onions hinders blood clotting and may help prevent heart attacks. Other studies indicate that both onions and garlic may protect against the artery-clotting damage of elevated blood cholesterol.

More ideas

• Scallop and orange sauté: For the shrimp, substitute 1¼ pounds sea scallops, cooking them about 4 minutes or just until they turn opaque (step 5). Substitute 2 cups fresh orange sections for the pineapple chunks (step 6).

• Spicy fish satay: Substitute ⅓ cup crunchy peanut butter (step 3) for the cream of coconut. Substitute 1¼ pounds skinless flounder, snapper, or cod fillets, cut into bite-size pieces, for the shrimp (step 5).

savory ways with fruit

Chicken with apricots and cumin

Chicken thighs are one of the most flavorful parts of the chicken. Simmer them up with Far Eastern spices of cumin and coriander, plus crunchy fennel and delicate, fresh apricots. Or, create a similar dish made with slimming skinless chicken breasts and fresh oranges. Serve with fragrant saffron rice.

Makes 6 servings

6 large chicken thighs (about 2 pounds)

2 tablespoons sunflower oil

1 large yellow onion, sliced (1 cup)

2 large garlic cloves, minced

2 teaspoons ground coriander

2 teaspoons ground cumin

½ teaspoon salt

¼ teaspoon freshly ground black pepper

1⅓ cups low-fat chicken stock

4 large carrots, peeled, halved crosswise, then each cut lengthwise into 8 "fingers"

1 bulb of fennel, halved lengthwise, then cut crosswise into ¼ inch thick slices (reserve the leaves for decorating)

12 ounces ripe but firm apricots, pitted and quartered (about 6 large)

Preparation time: 15 minutes

Cooking time: 50 minutes

Each serving (without skin) provides

calories 398, total fat 20g, saturated fat 5g, cholesterol 125mg, sodium 416mg, total carbohydrate 17g, dietary fiber 3g, protein 41g

✓✓✓	A, niacin
✓✓	B₆, C, potassium, zinc
✓	B₁, B₂, iron, magnesium, copper, fiber

1 Remove the skin from the chicken thighs, if you wish. In a large heavy Dutch oven or deep skillet, heat oil over medium-high heat. Add the chicken thighs and fry for 8 minutes or until golden brown all over, turning them occasionally. Transfer the thighs to a wire rack to drain.

2 To the same pan, add the onion and garlic and sauté for 7 minutes or until soft and golden. Stir in the coriander, cumin, salt, and pepper. Cook 1 minute more, then whisk in the stock.

3 Return the chicken to the Dutch oven, adding the carrots and fennel. Bring to a boil, then reduce the heat to low. Cover and simmer gently for 30 minutes or until the chicken is tender and the juices run clear when a thigh is pierced with a fork. Remove the cover. If there is too much liquid, increase the heat to high and boil the mixture a few minutes, to reduce the liquid slightly.

4 Add the apricots (do not peel) to the casserole and stir gently to mix. Simmer over low heat 5 minutes more or until the apricots are tender. Decorate with the reserved fennel leaves. Serve the dish with saffron rice (see page 66) or parsleyed mashed potatoes, plus a salad of endive, ruby red grapefruit sections, and green onions, tossed with a white wine vinaigrette.

Healthy tips

● Chicken is an excellent source of high-quality protein.

● Both apricots and carrots provide beta-carotene, which the body converts to vitamin A. The carrots are by far the better source, providing about ten times more beta-carotene than apricots. Vitamin A is essential for maintaining good vision. Plus, this vitamin is increasingly recognized as an important antioxidant, helping to prevent cancer and coronary heart disease.

More ideas

● Chicken cutlets with fresh oranges: In place of the chicken thighs, substitute 6 boneless, skinless chicken breast cutlets, about 2 pounds (step 1). Substitute 2 cups of fresh orange sections for the apricots (step 4).

● Apricot chicken with black bean sauce: Omit the ground coriander and cumin (step 2) and add ½ cup bottled black bean sauce after the chicken is cooked (end of step 3). Heat through.

savory ways with fruit

Lamb and fig stew with star anise

Take a tip from Mediterranean chefs and discover great meat and fruit creations. Here, bites of tender lamb simmer with sweet figs, fresh vegetables, and warm spices to create a stew that's hearty, savory, and satisfying. With a chunk of sourdough, you have supper. Another day, make it with beef and apricots.

Makes 6 servings

2 tablespoons olive oil

3 large garlic cloves, minced

3 large yellow onions, thinly sliced (3 cups)

2 pounds boneless leg of lamb, trimmed

1 cup ready-to-eat dried figs (5½ ounces)

1½ tablespoons grated fresh gingerroot

1 cinnamon stick, broken in half

2 star anise or 1 teaspoon anise seeds

1 pound carrots

1 pound zucchini

⅓ cup bottled chili sauce

¼ teaspoon salt

½ teaspoon freshly ground black pepper

¾ cup chopped fresh parsley

¾ cup chopped fresh coriander

Saffron rice

2 cups basmati rice

Large pinch saffron threads or ground saffron

½ teaspoon salt

Preparation time: 1 hour
Cooking time: 2 hours

Each serving provides
calories 569, **total fat** 12g, **saturated fat** 3g, **cholesterol** 65mg, **sodium** 575mg, **total carbohydrate** 88g, **dietary fiber** 7g, **protein** 31g

✓✓✓	A, niacin, C
✓✓	B₁, B₂, B₆, B₁₂, iron, potassium, zinc, fiber
✓	folate, calcium, magnesium, copper

1. Heat the olive oil in a 6-quart Dutch oven or saucepot over medium-high heat. Add the garlic and sauté for 1 minute or until it turns opaque. Stir in the onions, coating them with the oil. Reduce the heat to low, cover tightly, and simmer (without peeking) for 20 minutes or until the onions are very tender and sweet.

2. While the onions cook, cut the lamb into 1½-inch chunks. Add the lamb to the onions and pour in 6 cups of water. Increase the heat to high and bring to a boil, skimming off any foam. Then, reduce the heat to low and stir in the figs, gingerroot, cinnamon stick, and star anise. Cover the stew and simmer for 1 hour or until the meat is very tender.

3. While the stew simmers, put the rice in a bowl, cover with water, and soak for 30 minutes. Drain well.

4. While the rice soaks, peel and cut the carrots into 1½-inch chunks; cut the zucchini (do not peel) into 1½-inch chunks; set aside. Heat a small dry saucepan over high heat about 1 minute or until hot. Add the saffron and toast, stirring, for 30 seconds or until fragrant. Transfer the saffron to a heatproof bowl and pour in 2 cups of boiling water. Stir to mix, then let stand to infuse for 30 minutes.

5. When the lamb is tender, transfer it with a slotted spoon from the Dutch oven to a bowl; set aside. Discard the star anise (if using) and the cinnamon stick. Transfer about 1 cup of the vegetables and 1 cup of the liquid to a food processor or blender; process 1 minute or until smooth. Stir this onion mixture back into the stew in the Dutch oven, thickening the sauce.

6. Return the lamb to the Dutch oven, stir in the carrots, and bring to a boil. Reduce the heat to low and simmer, uncovered, for 10 minutes.

7. Add the zucchini to the stew and continue simmering for 5 minutes or until the vegetables are tender yet still crisp. Then cook the stew over low heat while you steam the rice. If the sauce for the stew is the thickness you want, cover the pan while you cook the rice; if it's too thin, continue cooking, uncovered, until it's the thickness you want.

8. To cook the rice, pour the saffron-infused water into a heavy medium-size saucepan, add the salt, and bring to a boil over high heat. Stir in the rice and return to a boil. Reduce the heat to low, cover the saucepan, and simmer for 10 minutes. Remove the rice from the heat and let stand, covered, 5 minutes more.

savory ways with fruit

savory ways with fruit

9 Taste the stew and stir in the chili sauce, salt, and pepper. Adjust the seasonings, if you wish. Sprinkle the stew with the chopped parsley and coriander, and serve immediately, with the saffron rice on the side.

More ideas

• Lamb and apricot stew: Substitute 1 cup of chopped dried apricots or chopped dried pitted dates for the figs (step 2).

• Beef and apricot stew: Substitute 2 pounds of lean boneless beef chuck steak for the lamb (step 2). In place of the figs, use 1½ cups chopped dried apricots (step 2). Stir 1 tablespoon Worcestershire sauce into the stew with the carrots (step 6).

• Vegetarian stew: For the lamb, substitute 1½ pounds small red-skinned potatoes, cut in half (step 2); cook 30 minutes instead of 1 hour. With the carrots, add a 1-pound can of drained cannellini beans (step 6).

Healthy tips

• Lamb tends to contain more fat than other meats. Recent changes in breeding, feeding, and processing mean that today's lean cuts of lamb contain only about one-third of the fat they had 20 years ago. More of the fat is monounsaturated, which is good news for keeping hearts healthy.

Pork chops with Asian pears

Start with boneless loin chops, then flavor them with hoisin sauce, soy, and ginger wine. Grill them to perfection, with rings of sweet and juicy Asian (Chinese) pears alongside. To complete the menu, steam up fragrant basmati rice with Chinese five-spice powder and more chunks of Asian pears.

Makes 4 servings

Marinade

¼ cup fresh orange juice

2 tablespoons low-sodium soy sauce

1 tablespoon hoisin sauce

1 tablespoon ginger wine

Grilled chops & pears

4 boneless pork loin chops, 1 inch thick, well trimmed of fat, about 5 ounces each (1¼ pounds)

1 extra-large Asian pear (about 8 ounces)

Sprigs of fresh coriander, for garnish

Oriental rice

1 cup basmati rice

2¼ cups water

2 thin slices fresh gingerroot, peeled

2 teaspoons Chinese five-spice powder

¼ teaspoon anise seeds

2 tablespoons (¼ stick) unsalted butter

¼ teaspoon salt

½ teaspoon freshly ground black pepper

2 large Asian pears, peeled, cored and chopped (about 12 ounces)

2 tablespoons finely chopped fresh coriander

Preparation time: 30 minutes

Marinating, soaking, and infusing: at least 1¾ hours

Cooking time: 20 minutes

Grilling or broiling time: 10 minutes

1 To make the marinade, mix the orange juice, soy sauce, hoisin sauce, and ginger wine in a dish large enough to hold the pork chops in a single layer. Add the chops, turning them to coat on both sides. Cover with plastic wrap and marinate the chops in the refrigerator for at least 1 hour, preferably up to 12 hours.

2 To prepare the rice, rinse it in a strainer under cold running water until the water runs clear. Place rice in a bowl and add enough water to cover at least 1 inch. Soak for 30 minutes.

3 In a small saucepan, combine the 2¼ cups water, the gingerroot, five-spice powder, and anise seeds and bring to a full boil over high heat. Remove from the heat, cover, and let stand for 30 minutes to infuse the water.

4 Using a slotted spoon, remove the spices from the water; bring the water back to a boil. Drain the rice well. In a large heavy saucepan, melt the butter over medium-high heat. Add the rice and stir until it is well coated. Pour in the boiling spice-infused water and add the salt and pepper. Reduce the heat to low and stir in the chopped Asian pears. Cover and simmer for 10 minutes. Remove from the heat and let stand, without stirring, for 5 minutes.

5 While the rice is cooking, grill or broil the chops. Lightly oil the grill or broiler rack and preheat the grill (or broiler). Peel, core, and cut the Asian pear into 4 rings, ½ inch thick. Remove the pork chops from the marinade. In a small saucepan, bring the marinade to a boil. Cook the chops, about 6 inches from the heat, for 5 minutes, basting with some marinade.

6 Turn the chops over and place the Asian pear rings next to the chops. Continue cooking and basting 5 minutes more or until the chops are done the way you like them and the juices run clear when the center of a chop is pierced with the tip of a sharp knife. Turn the pear rings over halfway through the cooking time.

7 Uncover the rice and stir in the chopped coriander. Taste and adjust the seasonings, if necessary. Serve each chop with a large portion of the spiced rice. Garnish each chop with an Asian pear ring and sprigs of coriander.

Each serving (1 lean chop) provides

calories 421, total fat 16g, saturated fat 7g, cholesterol 65mg, sodium 593mg, total carbohydrate 52g, dietary fiber 0g, protein 21g

✓✓	B_1, niacin
✓	B_2, B_6, C, iron, potassium, zinc

More ideas

• Asian chicken: Replace the pork chops with 4 flattened, skinless boneless chicken breasts, each weighing about 5 ounces (1¼ pounds total). Marinate the chicken breasts as in step 1, then grill for 6 minutes on each side or until the juices run clear when the chicken is pierced with the tip of a knife. Cook rice in chicken stock instead of spiced water.

• Pork méditerranéen: Make the marinade with 4 ounces dry red wine (½ cup), 1 large crushed garlic clove, 4 shredded fresh sage leaves, and 2 thin strips of lemon zest (step 1). Omit step 3. Steam the rice without the spices (step 4) and substitute 2 large, peeled chopped peaches for the Asian pears (step 4); stir in chopped fresh parsley instead of the coriander (step 7). Garnish with parsley sprigs.

Healthy tips

• Pork is an excellent source of high-quality protein and one of the best sources for thiamine (B_1), needed to metabolize energy.

• Despite pork's rather fatty image of the past, the fat content of today's lean pork is around 4%, lower than that of beef or lamb.

Prune and prosciutto kebabs with apricot sauce

Thread plump prunes wrapped in paper-thin slices of prosciutto onto skewers with onion wedges and yellow pepper squares. Grill them and serve with a piquant apricot sauce. Add a green salad and you have supper.

Makes 4 servings (2 kebabs each)

Kebabs

24 large pitted fresh or dried ready-to-eat prunes

12 very thin slices prosciutto (Parma ham), (4 ounces)

4 medium onions, each cut lengthwise into 6 wedges (12 ounces)

3 yellow bell peppers, seeded and cut into 24 squares (1½-inch squares)

2 tablespoons sunflower oil

Apricot sauce

1 15¼-ounce can unpeeled apricot halves in light or heavy syrup, undrained

2 green onions, both white and green parts, chopped (¼ cup)

½ teaspoon ground cumin

1 teaspoon low-sodium soy sauce

1 teaspoon balsamic vinegar

To serve (optional)

Cooked bulghur, rice pilaf, or saffron rice (page 66)

4 green onions, cut into thin shreds

Preparation time: 30 minutes

Cooking time (sauce): 8 minutes

Grilling or broiling time (kebabs): 8 minutes

1 If using dried pitted prunes, cook and plump them in boiling water, then drain them well, according to package directions. Cut each slice of prosciutto in half, or into thirds if large, and wrap a piece around each prune. Thread the prosciutto-wrapped prunes onto 8 skewers, alternating with the onion wedges and bell pepper squares.

2 To make the apricot sauce, put the apricots with their syrup, the green onions, and cumin in a saucepan. Bring just to a boil, reduce heat to medium-low, and simmer, uncovered, for 5 minutes. Pour into a food processor or blender, add the soy sauce and vinegar and blend until smooth. Set aside.

3 If you wish, make the rice or pasta: prepare a seasoned bulghur, rice, or pilaf mix according to the package directions. Or prepare the saffron rice (see page 66). Keep warm.

4 To cook the kebabs, preheat the grill or broiler to high. Brush the kebabs with the oil and cook, 6 inches from the heat, for 8 minutes, turning until peppers and onions are tender. Meanwhile, reheat the apricot sauce. Serve 2 kebabs per person with a generous spoonful of apricot sauce, plus shredded green onions, if you wish.

Healthy tips

• Ounce per ounce, bell peppers are a better source of vitamin C than citrus fruits. Plus, they are low in calories.

• Prunes are a popular remedy for preventing constipation, thanks to their high dietary fiber content and isatin, a natural laxative. Prunes are also rich in iron. The vitamin C from the apricots in the sauce helps the body absorb the iron.

Another idea

• Turkey and nectarine kebabs: Substitute 4 large unpeeled nectarines for the prunes and 4 ounces smoked turkey slices for the prosciutto. Cut the nectarines in half and pit them (do not peel). Cut each half lengthwise into 3 equal wedges. Wrap the nectarines with the turkey as in step 1.

Each serving (2 kebabs) provides

calories 333, total fat 9g, saturated fat 1g, cholesterol 16mg, sodium 437mg, total carbohydrate 58g, dietary fiber 7g, protein 11g

✓✓✓	C
✓✓	B₆, potassium, fiber
✓	A, B₁, B₂, niacin, iron, magnesium, copper

savory ways with fruit

70

Thai stir-fried steak with mango

Most Thai dishes, especially this one, are bursting with fresh flavors and deliciously contrasting textures. The dressing is completely oil-free. Even though both the steak and nuts contain fat and the beef is stir-fried in a little oil, the dish is surprisingly low in fat. Also, no extra salt is needed, due to the spicy dressing and soy sauce.

Makes 4 servings

Dressing

¼ cup rice vinegar or cider vinegar

2 tablespoons golden honey

2 teaspoons mild chili powder

2 teaspoons paprika

1 tablespoon grated fresh gingerroot

¾ cup water

3 tablespoons fresh lime or lemon juice

Salad

2 large ripe mangoes

4 large ripe juicy plums (about 1 pound)

3 cups watercress leaves (about 2 bunches)

½ medium red cabbage, shredded (1½ cups)

1 cup cucumber matchsticks (1 large)

1 cup thin red pepper strips (1 large)

4 green onions, cut in diagonal pieces

½ cup chopped fresh coriander

½ cup chopped fresh mint

2 tablespoons coarsely chopped roasted unsalted peanuts

Stir-fried beef steak

1 pound lean sirloin steak

2 teaspoons low-sodium soy sauce

3 large garlic cloves, minced

1 teaspoon sugar

1½ tablespoons sunflower oil

Preparation time: 45 minutes

Cooking time: about 10 minutes

1 First, make the dressing. In a small saucepan, whisk together the vinegar, honey, chili powder, paprika, and gingerroot. Slowly whisk in the water and bring to a boil over high heat. Reduce the heat to medium and simmer, uncovered, for 5 minutes. Remove from the heat and whisk in the lime juice. Set aside.

2 Peel the mangoes but not the plums. Cut the fruits in half, remove the pits, and thinly slice them, ¼ inch thick. Place in a large shallow bowl (you should have 5 cups). Add the watercress, cabbage, cucumber, red pepper, green onions, coriander, and mint. Toss gently to mix. Set aside.

3 Diagonally cut the steak into thin strips for stir-frying, ¼ inch thick. In a large bowl, coat the steak with 3 tablespoons of the dressing, the soy sauce, garlic, and sugar. Heat a wok or nonstick skillet over high heat, add the oil, then the steak. Stir-fry just until the steak strips are cooked to taste.

4 Spoon the stir-fried steak over the salad. Drizzle with the rest of the dressing and sprinkle with the peanuts.

More ideas

● Tropical Thai beef stir-fry: Increase the fruit by adding 2 cups fresh pineapple chunks or 1 cup peeled kiwi slices with the fruits (step 2).

● Thai stir-fried chicken with nectarines: Substitute 3 large ripe juicy nectarines for the mangoes (step 2). Substitute 1 pound boneless, skinless chicken breasts for the beef (step 3). Use a mallet to pound the chicken ⅜ inch thick before slicing diagonally into strips.

Healthy tips

● All orange and red fruits and vegetables, such as mangoes, red cabbage, and red peppers, are excellent sources of beta-carotene and vitamin C – both antioxidants that help to protect against heart disease and cancer. The vitamin C helps the body absorb valuable iron from the steak.

● Besides adding its delicious spiciness to the dressing, ginger also aids in digestion.

● Both beef and peanuts are excellent sources of protein. Peanuts, unlike beef, are cholesterol free.

Each serving provides

calories 427, **total fat** 14g, **saturated fat** 3g, **cholesterol** 65mg, **sodium** 187mg, **total carbohydrate** 52g, **dietary fiber** 7g, **protein** 27g

✓✓✓	C
✓✓	A, B₁, B₂, niacin, B₆, B₁₂, iron, potassium, zinc, fiber
✓	folate, calcium, magnesium, copper

savory ways with fruit

Roasted roots with apricots

Collect some of your favorite root vegetables at the market, such as carrots, sweet potatoes, and turnips. Brown them in hot oil and roast slowly with apricots and orange juice until they caramelize and cook to perfection.

Makes 4 side-dish servings

9 ounces dried apricots (1½ cups)

3 large shallots

8 ounces carrots (about 6 large)

8 ounces sweet potatoes (about 2 medium)

8 ounces turnips (about 2 medium)

1 medium-size celeriac (celery root)

4 ounces large white mushrooms

2 large yellow onions

2 tablespoons olive oil

1 cup vegetable or chicken stock

1 cup fresh orange juice

½ teaspoon coarsely ground black pepper

Sprigs of fresh parsley

To decorate (optional)

Sprig of fresh parsley

Preparation time: 45 minutes

Cooking time: 1 hour

Each side-dish serving provides ⓥ

calories 403, total fat 10g, saturated fat 1g, cholesterol 0mg, sodium 127mg, total carbohydrate 83g, dietary fiber 11g, protein 7g

✓✓✓	A, C, potassium
✓✓	B₆, iron, copper, fiber
✓	B₁, B₂, niacin, folate, calcium, magnesium

1 Place the apricots in a bowl and cover with boiling water. Let them soak for 15 minutes or until plump and juicy; drain well.

2 Preheat the oven to 350°F. Peel the shallots and quarter them lengthwise. Peel the carrots, sweet potatoes, and turnips; cut into 1½-inch chunks. Cut the celeriac into 2-inch chunks. Wash the mushrooms well and quarter them. Peel and cut the onions into thin slivers. You will have about 8 cups of vegetables.

3 In a 5- or 6-quart Dutch oven or deep flameproof casserole, heat the oil over medium-high heat. Stir in the shallots, carrots, sweet potatoes, turnips, celeriac, mushrooms, and onions, coating them lightly with the oil. Cook, stirring frequently, for 10 minutes or until the vegetables are golden brown.

4 Pour the vegetable stock and orange juice over the vegetables and bring to a boil. Add the apricots and the pepper. Transfer the Dutch oven (do not cover) to the oven and bake, uncovered, for 1 hour or until the vegetables are tender and the sauce has thickened. Decorate with parsley and serve with chunks of crusty bread, if you wish.

More ideas

● Far Eastern roasted roots: Before adding the vegetables to the heated oil (step 3), stir in 2 teaspoons ground cumin and 1 teaspoon garam masala; let cook 30 seconds, then add the vegetables as directed.

● Basque roasted roots: Substitute 1 cup beef stock for the vegetable or chicken stock and a 1-pound can of tomatoes (do not drain) for the orange juice (step 4).

Healthy tips

● Root vegetables are generally good sources of fiber. Carrots and sweet potatoes are excellent sources of beta-carotene, which the body converts to vitamin A. It's the vitamin that is essential for vision, healthy skin, and growth.

● Dried apricots also provide beta-carotene, along with iron, potassium, and fiber.

savory ways with fruit

Frijoles with fruit

This classic dish, from south-of-the-border down Mexico-way, pairs up earthy frijoles rojos pequeños *(small red beans) with juicy pineapple, green-skinned apples, and fresh tomato. The result is this Mexican bean dish,* frijoles con frutas. *Does fruit with beans sound alarming? Just remember that the tomato is also a fruit!*

Makes 4 servings

½ large fresh pineapple (about 1 pound)

2 large tart green-skinned apples, such as Granny Smith

2 tablespoons fresh lemon juice

2 tablespoons sunflower oil

2 large yellow onions, chopped (2 cups)

3 large garlic cloves, minced

3 large ripe tomatoes, diced (2 cups)

1 teaspoon hot chili powder or hot pepper sauce, or more to taste

¼ teaspoon salt

2 15-ounce cans *frijoles rojos pequeños* beans, well drained (4 cups beans)

To decorate

Fresh coriander sprigs

Preparation time: 30 minutes
Cooking time: 30 minutes

Each serving provides Ⓥ

calories 371, total fat 8g, saturated fat 1g, cholesterol 0mg, sodium 602mg, total carbohydrate 69g, dietary fiber 20g, protein 13g

✓✓✓	C, fiber
✓	B₁, B₆, folate, calcium, iron, potassium, copper

1 First, prepare the fruit. Peel the pineapple and cut out the core. Cut a few thin matchsticks of pineapple for the garnish and chop the rest into bite-size chunks (you need 3 cups). Core the apples (do not peel); cut half of one apple into thin slices for the garnish and cut the remaining 1½ apples into ½-inch dice. In a bowl, toss the fruit for the garnish with the lemon juice. Cover with plastic wrap and set aside.

2 In a large deep skillet, heat the oil over medium-high heat. Stir in the onions and garlic and sauté the vegetables for 7 minutes or until soft and golden. Add the diced apples and continue to cook for about 5 minutes, stirring frequently, until the apples are lightly browned. Stir in the pineapple chunks, cook 3 minutes more, then add the tomatoes, chili powder, and salt; bring to a simmer. Reduce the heat to low and cook the mixture, uncovered, for 15 minutes or until thickened.

3 Add the drained beans to the fruit in the pan and stir well. Continue to cook over a low heat for 10 minutes, stirring and mingling the flavors.

4 Decorate the beans and fruit with the reserved pineapple sticks and apple slices, plus the fresh coriander sprigs. Serve hot with warmed flour tortillas and a raw vegetable salad.

Healthy tips

• Tomatoes are well known as a good source of vitamin C. New research shows that tomatoes contain lycopene, a carotenoid that has been linked to reducing the risk of certain cancers, such as prostate cancer. Cooking enhances the absorption of lycopene by the body.

• Beans contain both soluble and insoluble fiber. Insoluble fiber provides roughage, which may lessen the risk of bowel cancer, and soluble fiber has been connected with lowering cholesterol levels in the blood, thus reducing the risk of heart disease and strokes.

Another idea

• *Lentejas costeñas con frutas* (Mexican lentils with fruit): Substitute lentils for the beans. In a large saucepan, combine 1 cup (5⅓ ounces) dried brown-green lentils (no soaking is needed) with 1 quart (4 cups) water, ½ teaspoon salt, and 2 bay leaves. Cook according to package directions for about 35 minutes or until tender, then rinse and drain the lentils (you should have 4 cups of cooked lentils). Add the lentils to the fruit mixture (step 3). Use hot pepper sauce instead of chili powder (step 2).

savory ways with fruit

Pears broiled with pecorino

From the countryside of Tuscany comes this traditional pairing of sweet juicy pears with savory pecorino cheese. Depending upon the pecorino you choose, it can be creamy and mild in flavor or hard and pungent. Melt some over the pears and toss other bites with sweet grapes in this arugula and watercress salad.

Makes 4 servings

Balsamic vinaigrette

⅓ cup extra virgin olive oil

3 tablespoons best-quality balsamic vinegar

1 teaspoon Dijon mustard

¾ teaspoon sugar

¼ teaspoon salt

¼ teaspoon freshly ground black pepper

Arugula fruit salad

4 ounces arugula, leaves removed from stems (6 cups)

1 bunch of watercress, about 2 ounces, leaves removed from stems (2 cups)

1 cup seedless green grapes, halved

3 ounces Italian pecorino cheese, made from sheep's milk (see selections at right)

2 large ripe dessert pears, such as Comice or red Bartlett

Preparation time: 20 minutes
Broiling time: about 2 minutes

Each serving (½ pear) provides Ⓥ

calories 342, **total fat** 24g, **saturated fat** 6g, **cholesterol** 22mg, **sodium** 469mg, **total carbohydrate** 26g, **dietary fiber** 4g, **protein** 9g

✓✓	calcium
✓	A, B₂, folate, C, magnesium, potassium, fiber

1 First, make the dressing. Put the oil, vinegar, mustard, sugar, salt, and pepper into a pint-size jar with a screw top. Cover and shake until well blended. Chill the dressing until you're ready to use it.

2 In a large salad bowl, toss the arugula, watercress, and green grapes. Using a vegetable peeler or cheese slicer, cut the pecorino cheese into very thin slices. Roughly chop half of the slices and toss into the salad bowl. Set aside the rest of the slices for melting on the pears.

3 Preheat the broiler to high. Cover the baking sheet with foil. Peel the pears, cut in half, and core.

4 Arrange the pear halves, cut-sides down, on the baking sheet. Top the pears with the reserved cheese slices, overlapping them. Broil the pears, 6 inches from the heat source, for 2 minutes or just until the cheese begins to bubble and turns golden. (Watch carefully, as it can burn easily!)

5 Meanwhile, shake the dressing, drizzle it over the salad, and toss until the leaves are coated. Mound the salad equally on 4 salad plates. Using a small spatula, carefully arrange one pear half on the top of each salad. Serve at once while the melted cheese is warm and the greens are still crisp.

More ideas

- From Italy come pecorino cheeses, which are made from sheep's milk.

— Pecorino Romano: hard yellow rind, yellowish-white interior, sharp and pungent in flavor, great for grating

— Pecorino Sardo: soft, salty, piquant

— Pecorino Siciliano: delicate, soft, creamy, especially when eaten freshly made

— Pecorino Toscano: whiter, more delicate, with a very creamy center

- Nectarines grilled with Gorgonzola: Substitute 4 ounces Gorgonzola for the pecorino. Using a serrated knife, slice the cheese as thin as possible. Toss half into the salad. Place the nectarines on the baking sheet cut-side up and stuff the cavities with the remaining cheese. Broil the nectarines just until the cheese melts.

- Raspberries with grilled Brie: Make the dressing with ⅓ cup raspberry vinegar instead of balsamic. Make the salad, substituting ½ pint (1 cup) ripe raspberries for the grapes and 4 ounces Brie for the pecorino. Stuff the cavities of the pears with the Brie and broil cut-side up.

Healthy tip

- This salad is a good source of calcium, needed for healthy bones and teeth. The pecorino cheese contributes 78% of the calcium; the watercress and arugula, 17%.

savory ways with fruit

Fast Fruit Desserts

Scrumptious sweets—quick to fix and delicious

FRESH FRUIT, such as a bowl of ripe raspberries with a scoop of frozen yogurt, is the fastest of fast desserts. But, with just a little time and a few extra ingredients, fruits can quickly turn into even more wonderful finales. Simmer dried cranberries and bananas into creamy rice pudding, bake fresh plums inside parchment packets, or grill fruits *en brochettes* and serve them with a fresh berry coulis. Many fast desserts are special enough for even the fanciest dinner parties. Flambé fresh pears with brandy, whirl and bake apricots into a puffy soufflé, or scoop out a bowlful of fresh berry fool, made with yogurt and cream. They're all fast, fabulous, and good for you!

Flambéed Asian pears with orange

An impressive dessert! Also known as Chinese pears or apple pears, the most common variety of Asian pear in the U.S. is the Twentieth Century. It's large, round, and yellowish-green. Look for these crunchy juicy pears from late summer through early fall. Simmer them up with oranges, then flambé them elegantly with brandy.

Makes 4 servings
(recipe can be doubled)

2 large Asian pears (about 1½ pounds)
2 to 3 tablespoons fresh lemon juice
3 large navel oranges
2 tablespoons (¼ stick) unsalted butter
3 tablespoons light brown sugar
3 tablespoons brandy

To decorate

3 tablespoons coarsely chopped pistachios
Sprigs of fresh lemon balm

Preparation time: 20 minutes
Cooking time: 10 minutes

Each serving provides 🅥

calories 267, total fat 9g, saturated fat 4g, cholesterol 15mg, sodium 5mg, total carbohydrate 45g, dietary fiber 4g, protein 3g

✓✓✓ C

✓ B₁, folate, magnesium, potassium, copper, fiber

1 Peel, quarter, and core the Asian pears. Cut them lengthwise into slices. To prevent the pears from turning brown, immediately sprinkle them with the lemon juice and toss until coated.

2 Peel the oranges, removing the white pith. Cut the oranges crosswise into slices, ¼ inch thick.

3 In a large skillet, melt the butter, over medium heat. Add the sugar, stirring constantly, so it doesn't burn. Quickly add the pear slices and cook gently for 3 minutes on each side or just until tender yet firm to the touch. Add the orange slices and cook 1 minute more or just until warmed and well coated with the juices in the skillet.

4 Using a slotted spoon, transfer the pears and oranges to a shallow serving dish and keep warm. Increase the heat to high and boil the juices in the uncovered skillet until reduced to about half, then pour over the fruit. Pour the brandy into the frying pan, heat it, stand back, and ignite. Pour over the fruits.

5 Serve the flambéed fruits on 4 warmed plates. Sprinkle with the pistachios and decorate with the sprigs of lemon balm.

More ideas

• Flambéed pineapple with orange: Substitute 3 cups fresh pineapple spears for the Asian pears (step 1). Flambé with 3 tablespoons dark rum in place of the brandy and sprinkle with 3 tablespoons chopped toasted pecans instead of the pistachios (step 5).

• Flambéed Comice pears with orange: Substitute 3 large Comice pears for the Asian pears. Cook only 2 minutes on each side or just until tender (step 3). Then add the oranges and continue as directed. Flambé with Poire William instead of the brandy (step 4).

• Flambéed apples with Calvados: Substitute 3 large, peeled, cored Granny Smith apple slices for the pears. Flambé with Calvados instead of the brandy and sprinkle with chopped toasted hazelnuts (step 4).

Healthy tip

• Oranges are famous for their vitamin C content, a water-soluble vitamin that the body doesn't store. Consequently, it is essential that we eat fruits and vegetables containing vitamin C every day. Scientists are increasingly recognizing that the powerful antioxidant activity of vitamin C protects the body against cell damage by free radicals and may reduce the risk of certain cancers, heart attacks, and strokes.

Grilled fruit *en brochettes*

The French term en brochettes *refers to food cooked on skewers. Here, fresh fruits are grilled on skewers just long enough to heat the fruits and caramelize the sugars, making a wonderful dessert. Be careful not to leave the brochettes on the grill too long, as fruits can over-brown quickly. These are best served right off the grill.*

Makes 8 brochettes or 4 servings

Brochettes

8 bamboo skewers, 10 to 12 inches long

Raspberry-orange coulis

1 pint fresh raspberries (2 cups)

1½ teaspoons grated orange zest

½ cup fresh orange juice

2 tablespoons sugar

Fruits en brochettes

4 fresh figs, or 4 dried figs, soaked and
   drained (½ pound)

½ large fresh pineapple (1 pound)

2 large pears, ripe but firm (1 pound)

2 large peaches, ripe but firm (1 pound)

2 large bananas, ripe but firm

⅓ cup fresh lemon juice

⅓ cup sugar

Cape gooseberries or fresh raspberries

Preparation time: 30 minutes

Cooking time: 7 minutes

Each serving (2 brochettes) provides Ⓥ

calories 426, total fat 2g, saturated fat 0g,
cholesterol 0mg, sodium 4mg, total
carbohydrate 109g, dietary fiber 14g, protein 4g

✓✓✓	C, fiber
✓✓	B₆, potassium, copper
✓	B₁, B₂, niacin, folate, iron, magnesium

1 Soak the bamboo skewers in cold water for 20 minutes.

2 Meanwhile, make the coulis. In a blender or food processor, purée the raspberries, the orange zest and juice, and the sugar. Strain the mixture to remove the seeds, if you wish, but it's not absolutely necessary. Set aside.

3 Preheat the grill or broiler. Cut the figs lengthwise into four equal pieces (about 2 cups). Peel, core, and cut the pineapple into bite-size chunks (3 cups). Core (do not peel) the pears and cut into 1½-inch cubes. Pit (do not peel) the peaches and cut into 1½-inch cubes. Peel the bananas and cut crosswise into 1½-inch pieces. Thread the fruit onto the soaked skewers, alternating them to make a colorful arrangement. Mix the lemon juice and sugar in a cup. Baste the brochettes with half of the mixture; set aside the rest.

4 Grill the brochettes for 4 minutes on each side or until light golden brown. Turn the brochettes, baste with the remaining lemon juice mixture, and grill another 3 or 4 minutes or until light golden brown.

5 For each serving, spread about ⅓ cup coulis on a plate and arrange 2 fruit brochettes on top. Garnish with the gooseberries or raspberries, if you wish. Serve hot.

Healthy tips

• This delicious recipe provides an excellent amount of the antioxidant nutrient vitamin C, which comes from the pineapple, the raspberries, and the orange and lemon juices. A little beta-carotene, which the body converts to vitamin A, is provided by the peaches. Additionally, bananas are an excellent source of potassium, important in muscle functioning.

• Plenty of dietary fiber, essential for keeping the digestive tract healthy, is present in this array of fruit. Pectin, a soluble dietary fiber, regulates intestinal functions and can help to reduce blood cholesterol levels. Cellulose, an insoluble fiber, provides bulk and prevents constipation by promoting normal functioning of the intestines.

More ideas

• Fall fruit brochettes: Substitute 1 pound red-skinned apples, such as Cortland, Rome Beauty, or York Imperial (do not peel), for the peaches. Use 1 pound plums (do not peel) for the figs and omit the bananas.

• For appetizers, serve uncooked brochettes.

• Fruit market substitutes: For peaches, substitute the same amount of ripe nectarines. Fresh figs are available only from June through October in most markets. To use dried figs instead, soak and drain per package directions.

Hot apricot soufflés

It's easy to impress your guests with these delicate desserts. Start with a can of apricots, add a few eggs, a little milk and cream, plus some flavorings. After just 15 minutes in the oven, the batter puffs into light golden fluffs of heavenly ecstasy. Another day, make them with fresh strawberries or raspberries. You'll be glad you did.

Makes 4 individual soufflés

2 tablespoons ground almonds

1 15½-ounce can apricot halves in light
   syrup, well drained

⅓ cup granulated sugar, plus 2 tablespoons

3 tablespoons all-purpose flour

2 tablespoons whole milk

2 tablespoons heavy cream

3 large eggs, separated

2 tablespoons (¼ stick) unsalted butter,
   cut into pieces

1 tablespoon pure vanilla extract

1 teaspoon fresh lemon juice

1 large egg white

½ teaspoon cream of tartar

To finish

2 tablespoons confectioners' sugar

1 tablespoon unsweetened cocoa

Preparation time: 30 minutes

Baking time: 15 minutes

Each soufflé provides   Ⓥ

calories 352, total fat 15g, saturated fat 7g,
cholesterol 186mg, sodium 74mg, total
carbohydrate 48g, dietary fiber 2g, protein 8g

✓✓	A
✓	B₂, C, potassium

1 Set a baking sheet on the middle rack in the oven and preheat to 400°F. Butter four 10-ounce soufflé dishes, each 4" wide and 2½" high. Dust with the ground almonds. Purée the drained apricots in a food processor and set aside.

2 In a medium-size saucepan, mix the ⅓ cup sugar and the flour. Whisk in the milk and cream until well blended. Stir the sauce constantly over medium-high heat until it boils and thickens, then remove from the heat.

3 Using an electric mixer, beat the 3 egg yolks in a small bowl on high until thick and light yellow. Beat in a little of the hot sauce, then return the mixture to the pan. Whisk over medium heat for 2 minutes (do not boil). Remove from the heat and blend in the butter, then the apricot purée, vanilla, and lemon juice.

4 Beat the 4 egg whites and the cream of tartar in a clean bowl with clean beaters on high until stiff peaks form. Gently fold the whites into the apricot mixture. Divide the mixture among the soufflé dishes.

5 Bake the soufflés on the baking sheet for 15 minutes or until puffed and golden brown. Mix confectioners' sugar and cocoa and sift over the soufflés. Serve the soufflés immediately.

Healthy tips

• When buying canned fruit, choose those canned in natural juice or light syrup, not in heavy syrup. They have at least 15% less sugar and fewer calories.

• Eggs are a complete protein — an essential nutrient for good health.

More ideas

• Fresh strawberry soufflés: Omit the apricots. Purée 1 quart (4 cups) ripe hulled strawberries (you will have about 1¾ cups of purée). Use 1 cup of this purée in the soufflé batter (end of step 3). Bake the soufflés as directed. If you wish, stir 1 tablespoon framboise (raspberry liqueur) into the remaining strawberry purée. Right before serving the soufflés, gently push the tip of a spoon into the center of each and pour in some of the remaining purée.

• Hot raspberry soufflés: Omit the apricots. Purée 1 pint (2 cups) ripe raspberries (you will have about 1 cup of purée). Use this purée in the soufflé batter (end of step 3). Bake the soufflés as directed.

• Save the fruit juice or light syrup from the canned apricots; toss with a fresh fruit salad.

• Use a round-bladed knife to gently mark a circle in the center of each soufflé; this helps the tops to rise evenly.

Saffron and vanilla grilled fruit

Pick a collection of luscious fruits, spice them elegantly with saffron and vanilla, then grill them until the fruits release some of their juices and they are warm and fragrant. Top with a fruit sorbet or vanilla bean ice cream.

Makes 4 servings

Saffron marinade

1 small pinch of saffron threads or
⅛ teaspoon ground saffron
¼ cup hot water
⅓ cup fresh orange juice
2 tablespoons Marsala wine or sweet sherry
2 teaspoons pure vanilla extract
1 tablespoon golden honey

Salad

1 large papaya
1 Ugli fruit or 2 large navel oranges
2 large kiwis
2 large bananas
1 cup seedless black or purple grapes

To serve (optional)

4 scoops vanilla bean ice cream, lemon or
raspberry sorbet, or frozen vanilla yogurt

Preparation time: 15 minutes
Marinating time (optional): 1 hour
Grilling time: 5 minutes

Each serving provides Ⓥ

calories 229, total fat 1g, saturated fat 0g,
cholesterol 0mg, sodium 8mg, total
carbohydrate 55g, dietary fiber 6g, protein 3g

✓✓✓	C
✓✓	B₆, folate, potassium, fiber
✓	A, B₁, B₂, magnesium, copper

1 First, make the marinade. Heat a small dry saucepan over high heat about 1 minute or until hot. Add the saffron and toast, stirring, for 30 seconds or until fragrant. Chop the saffron finely or place in a mortar and crush it with a pestle. Place the saffron in a medium-size bowl and pour in the hot water. Stir in the orange juice, Marsala wine, vanilla, and honey.

2 Prepare the fruits, adding them to the marinade as you go. Peel the papaya, remove the seeds, and cut into bite-size chunks. Using a serrated fruit knife, peel the Ugli fruit or the oranges, removing all the white pith; cut between the membranes and lift out the sections.

3 Peel the kiwis, then cut each lengthwise into 6 wedges. Peel the bananas, half them lengthwise, then cut into bite-size chunks. Add the grapes. You will have about 8 cups of fruit. Stir gently to coat the fruit with the marinade. If time permits, let the fruit marinate for 1 hour before cooking.

4 Preheat the grill. Pour the fruit and marinade into a shallow ovenproof dish. Spread out the fruit in an even layer. Grill for 5 minutes or until all the fruit is heated through (or sauté fruit in a large skillet over medium-high heat for 5 minutes). Ladle the fruit into 4 fruit dishes. Serve warm with a scoop of ice cream, sorbet, or yogurt.

Healthy tips

• Papaya, Ugli fruit, and kiwis are excellent sources of vitamin C, which helps to heal wounds, strengthen blood vessel walls, and build teeth and bones. This vitamin also increases iron absorption, helps control blood cholesterol, and helps prevent atherosclerosis.

• The bananas, kiwis, and citrus fruits provide potassium, which keeps body fluids and blood pressure in balance.

• Papaya supplies beta-carotene, which the body makes into vitamin A, the nutrient needed for good vision. It is also important in maintaining healthy skin, hair, and nails.

More ideas

• Tropical grilled fruit: Omit the Ugli fruit and grapes. Substitute 2 cups fresh pineapple chunks and 2 cups of unpeeled plum slices. For the tropical marinade, use ⅓ cup fresh lime juice, 2 tablespoons white rum, 1 tablespoon golden honey, 2 teaspoons vanilla extract, and 1 teaspoon ground cinnamon. Sprinkle with seeds from 1 large pomegranate.

• Summer grilled fruit: Substitute 2 cups peeled fresh peach or nectarine slices for the kiwis and 1 cup pitted Bing cherries, cut in half, for the grapes.

• Ugli fruit from Jamaica is a large hybrid citrus fruit that's a cross between a grapefruit, orange, and tangerine. You'll find it in gourmet shops.

fast fruit desserts

89

Plums *en papillote* with honey

The French term en papillote *refers to baking foods in packets of parchment, sealing in all of the delicious juices. Look for baking parchment at a gourmet store or specialty cookware shop. The packets puff in the oven and look impressive. When opened, a wonderful spicy aroma is released and every bite is infused with flavor.*

Makes 4 individual papillotes

1 large juice orange, such as Valencia
4 squares baking parchment paper
   (14"x14")
8 large ripe dessert plums, pitted and sliced
   ½ inch thick (8 cups, about 1 pound)
2 tablespoons (¼ stick) unsalted butter,
   cut into 8 pieces
2 cinnamon sticks, halved
8 whole cloves
¼ cup golden honey

To serve

4 small scoops frozen vanilla yogurt or
   low-fat ice cream (½ pint)
3 tablespoons coarsely chopped pecans,
   preferably toasted
2 tablespoons honey for drizzling (optional)

Preparation time: 20 minutes
Cooking time: 20 minutes

Each papillote provides   Ⓥ

calories 384, total fat 15g, saturated fat 7g,
cholesterol 25mg, sodium 60mg, total
carbohydrate 61g, dietary fiber 4g, protein 6g

✓✓✓	C
✓✓	B₂
✓	A, B₁, B₆, B₁₂, folate, E, calcium, magnesium, potassium, fiber

1 Preheat the oven to 400°F and set out a large shallow pan with sides. Using a citrus zester or vegetable peeler, remove the zest from the orange; cut into thin shreds. Juice the orange (you need ½ cup of juice). Set aside.

2 For each of the 4 papillote packets, lay out a square of parchment. Spoon one-fourth of the plum slices in the center. Add 2 pieces of the butter, a piece of cinnamon stick, and 2 whole cloves. Drizzle with 1 tablespoon of honey. Top the plums with 3 or 4 strips of orange zest and drizzle with 2 tablespoons orange juice.

3 For each papillote, bring two opposite sides of the parchment paper together over the fruit filling and fold two or three times. Fold over the other opposite ends twice, tucking them under, to make a neatly sealed packet.

4 Place the packets in the baking pan, folded-ends up. Bake for 20 minutes or until the packets are slightly puffed and light brown. The fruit inside will be bubbling hot.

5 Place the packets on 4 individual dessert plates. Carefully open up each one (stand back to let the steam escape). Discard the whole cloves. Top each with a scoop of frozen yogurt and 2 teaspoons pecans. Drizzle with extra honey, if you wish. Serve immediately.

More ideas

● Fresh pineapple and banana *en papillote:* For the plums, substitute 1 small ripe pineapple, peeled, cored and cut into bite-size wedges, and 2 bananas, sliced ½ inch thick. Proceed as directed in step 2.

● Toffee papillotes: Substitute ¼ cup pure maple syrup for the honey.

● Plums and clementines *en papillote:* Substitute 5 fresh medium-size clementines (sweet, bright orange, thin-skinned, seedless oranges) for 4 of the plums. Peel, section, and mix with the plums.

Healthy tips

● Plums contain a fair amount of vitamin E, an important antioxidant that recent studies indicate may protect against some conditions associated with aging.

● Pecans, like other nuts, are rich in fat, but at least three-fourths of this fat is unsaturated. They also provide generous amounts of vitamin E.

● Yogurt, along with other dairy products, is a valuable source of calcium. This mineral is essential for the structure of bones and teeth, which contain 99% of all calcium in the body. But calcium is also important in a number of other vital processes, including blood clotting and the proper functioning of muscles and nerves.

fast fruit desserts

Glazed banana *pain perdu*

French toast in Creole country is called pain perdu, *meaning "lost bread." It's made from day-old "forgotten" bread.* Pain perdu *gives new dimensions to French toast, with its flavors and its caramelized bananas on top. Another day, try citrus fruits. For puffier toast, soak overnight.*

Makes 8 servings

8 slices firm day-old white toasting bread, ½ inch thick (1 ounce each)

3 large eggs

¼ cup low-fat milk (2% milkfat)

2 tablespoons golden honey

1 teaspoon pure vanilla extract

¼ teaspoon ground cinnamon

¼ cup (½ stick) unsalted butter

3 large bananas

To glaze

¼ cup sifted confectioners' sugar

¼ teaspoon ground cinnamon

To decorate (optional)

Sprigs of mint

Confectioners' sugar for dusting

Preparation time: 10 minutes

Standing time: 30 minutes or overnight

Cooking time: 12 minutes

Broiling time: 2 minutes

Each serving (1 slice bread) provides Ⓥ
calories 240, total fat 10g, saturated fat 5g, cholesterol 97mg, sodium 176mg, total carbohydrate 34g, dietary fiber 2g, protein 6g

✓   B₁, B₂, B₆

1 Trim the crusts off the bread and cut each slice diagonally into 2 equal triangles, making 16 pieces. Place the bread in a single layer in a large shallow dish. In a food processor or blender, place the eggs, milk, honey, vanilla, and cinnamon; process 2 minutes or until light yellow and frothy.

2 Pour the egg mixture over the bread triangles. Cover the dish with plastic wrap, refrigerate, and let stand for 30 minutes or overnight, turning the pieces of bread at least once.

3 Preheat the broiler and set out a baking sheet. In a large nonstick skillet, melt half of the butter over medium heat. Place half of the bread triangles in the skillet and cook for 3 minutes on each side until golden brown, then transfer to the baking sheet. Melt the remaining butter in the skillet; repeat, cooking the rest of the triangles.

4 Peel the bananas and cut them diagonally into thin slices, about ¼ inch thick. Arrange the banana slices on the toasts, overlapping the slices slightly. Mix the ¼ cup confectioners' sugar with the cinnamon and sprinkle over the bananas. Broil the toasts about 6 inches from the source of heat for 2 minutes or until the sugar melts and glazes the bananas.

5 To decorate, top the toasts with clusters of fresh mint and sprinkle a little extra confectioners' sugar on the leaves. Serve immediately.

More ideas

• Citrus *pain perdu*: Instead of the bananas, section 1 large ruby red grapefruit and 2 large navel oranges. For the glaze, substitute ⅓ cup light brown sugar for the confectioners' sugar. Drizzle with 1 tablespoon orange liqueur.

• Cinnamon-swirl raisin *pain perdu*: For the bread, use slices of cinnamon-swirl raisin bread. Substitute 2 cups peeled ripe peach slices for the bananas.

Healthy tips

• Contrary to popular belief, bread is not especially fattening; a 1-ounce slice of white, wheat, multigrain, or raisin bread contains only 65 calories. Often white bread is enriched with such nutrients as calcium, iron, thiamine, riboflavin, niacin, and folate.

• Eggs provide high-quality complete protein that supplies all the essential amino acids. Eggs do contain dietary cholesterol. Eggs are also an excellent source of vitamin B₁₂, essential for a healthy nervous system. The American Heart Association recommends eating up to 4 eggs each week.

fast fruit desserts

92

Peach & blackberry phyllo pizzas

Light, flaky, delicious, and very low in fat, phyllo (also filo) makes crisp, elegant pizza "shells." These simple attractive tarts have a delicate phyllo pastry base, ground almonds, and a luscious fresh fruit topping.

Makes 6 individual pizzas

5 sheets phyllo pastry, 14 "x 18 " each, thawed if frozen

¼ cup (½ stick) unsalted butter, melted

2 tablespoons ground almonds

3 large ripe peaches (about 1 pound)

½ pint fresh blackberries (1 cup)

¼ cup granulated sugar (preferably crystalline sanding sugar, see opposite page)

To serve (optional)

1 cup reduced-fat sour cream

3 tablespoons light brown sugar

Preparation time: 30 minutes

Baking time: 15 minutes

1 Preheat the oven to 400°F and butter a baking sheet. Lay out the 5 sheets of phyllo and immediately cover with plastic wrap, then a damp towel (phyllo dries out in a couple of minutes if left uncovered). Work fast!

2 Place a sheet of phyllo on the work surface and brush very lightly all over with about 2 teaspoons of the melted butter. Layer 4 more phyllo sheets, brushing with butter each time, and finally brushing the top sheet with the remaining butter. Using a 5" or 5½" saucer as a guide, cut out 6 circles from the layered phyllo. Transfer each layered circle to the baking sheet and sprinkle with the ground almonds.

3 To decorate, cut the peaches in half (do not peel), twist apart, and remove the pits. Slice the peaches very thin. Place the peach slices on the phyllo pastry circles in a pinwheel design. Divide the blackberries among the pizzas. Sprinkle 2 teaspoons sugar on top of each pizza.

4 Bake pizzas for 15 minutes or until the pastry is golden brown and the peaches are very tender and light brown. These pizzas are best served within 15 minutes, as the pastry can lose its crispness quickly if the fruit is juicy. If you wish, serve with sour cream sweetened with the brown sugar.

Healthy tips

● Even though the phyllo pastry is brushed with butter, the quantity used here is small compared to that normally used in similar phyllo preparations. Consequently, the total fat content in these pizzas is at least one-third lower than in tarts made with a buttery shortbread.

● Peaches are a source of vitamin A. They also contain fair amounts of vitamin C and potassium. Peaches are high in fiber, especially pectin, which is a soluble fiber that helps to lower high blood cholesterol. Fresh peaches are low in calories, with a medium-size peach containing only 35 calories.

● Blackberries provide an excellent source of vitamins C and E. These berries are also known for being rich in bioflavonoids, which work with vitamin C as antioxidants to boost immunity. Additionally, they contain ellagic acid, a substance that some experts believe helps prevent cancer.

Each pizza provides Ⓥ

calories 208, **total fat** 10g, **saturated fat** 5g, **cholesterol** 21mg, **sodium** 78mg, **total carbohydrate** 29g, **dietary fiber** 3g, **protein** 2g

✓ C, fiber

fast fruit desserts

94

More ideas

• Pear and raspberry phyllo pizzas: Substitute 1 pound ripe pears (preferably Red Bartletts) for the peaches; core the pears (do not peel) and slice 1/16 inch thick. Use 1/2 pint (1 cup) fresh raspberries instead of the blackberries.
If you wish, drizzle the pizzas with a little pear brandy after decorating and before sprinkling them with the sugar (end of step 3).

• Nectarine and raspberry phyllo pizzas: Substitute 1 pound ripe nectarines for the peaches (do not peel) and 1/2 pint (1 cup) fresh blueberries for the blackberries. Toss the sugar with 1/4 teaspoon ground cinnamon before sprinkling over the pizzas (end of step 3).
• Quick brandied peach pizzas: Substitute well-drained sliced peaches in brandy for the fresh peaches (no slicing time needed).

• Plum and raspberry phyllo pizzas: Use 1 pound ripe, pitted, unpeeled plums for the peaches. Slice 1/16 inch thick. Substitute 1/2 pint fresh raspberries for the blackberries. Drizzle the fruits with framboise (step 3).
• Crystalline sanding sugar, sold in gourmet stores, makes these pizzas glisten and sparkle. This sugar is sold in various sizes of crystals and usually does not melt away in the oven.

Cranberry and banana rice pudding

When making rice puddings, buy a short-grain rice, such as Italian arborio. This rice is so high in starch that it cooks up into a creamy milk pudding in less than 20 minutes. Dried bananas and cranberries add sweet 'n' natural fruit flavors. Golden raisins, dried cherries, and fresh raspberries make delicious pudding variations.

Serves 4

3½ cups low-fat milk (2% milkfat)

⅓ cup arborio rice or other short-grain, high-starch rice

¼ cup packed dark brown sugar

¼ cup granulated sugar

3 ounces dried cranberries (¾ cup)

1 ounce dried banana slices (¼ cup)

1 vanilla pod, split open in half or 1 teaspoon pure vanilla extract

To serve (optional)

Berry coulis (see page 25) or other fruit coulis

Scented geranium leaves for decoration

Preparation time: 15 minutes
Cooking time: 20 minutes
Chilling time (optional): 1 hour

1 Pour the milk into a heavy saucepan and stir in the rice, both of the sugars, the cranberries, bananas, and vanilla pod (if using).

2 Stirring constantly, cook the mixture over medium heat until it comes to a full boil. Reduce the heat to medium-low so the mixture is only gently simmering. Cook, stirring frequently, for 15 minutes or until the rice is swollen and tender and the pudding becomes thick and creamy.

3 Remove the pudding from the heat and remove the vanilla pod (or, if using vanilla extract instead, stir in at this point). Serve warm in large flat soup plates. If you wish, drizzle a few spoonfuls of a fresh berry coulis on top (see page 25) and decorate with scented, edible geranium leaves or edible flowers (see page 51). Tip: This pudding may also be made ahead of time and refrigerated. To serve, add a little extra milk and heat the pudding until it becomes creamy again.

More ideas

● Cinnamony rice and golden raisin pudding: Substitute 1 cup golden raisins (sultanas) for the dried cranberries and bananas; season with a 3-inch cinnamon stick instead of the vanilla pod (step 1).

● Creamy cherry-rice pudding: Substitute 1 cup dried cherries for the cranberries and bananas. Add a 3-inch cinnamon stick and ¼ teaspoon almond extract (step 1). Omit the vanilla pod.

● Raspberry-rice pudding: Substitute ½ pint (1 cup) fresh raspberries for the dried cranberries and bananas (step 1). If you wish, stir in 1 to 2 tablespoons framboise (raspberry liqueur) after cooking the pudding and after removing the vanilla pod (beginning of step 3).

Healthy tips

● Milk is one of our most nourishing foods. It is rich in calcium and vitamin D, which is essential for healthy teeth and bones, and is also a good source of protein. Milk is an excellent source of riboflavin (vitamin B_2), necessary for metabolizing energy.

● It is recommended that adults follow the guidelines for a healthy diet and switch to low-fat milk with 2% or 1% milkfat in order to reduce their intake of saturated fats.

● Cranberries, bananas, and rice all boost the carbohydrate content of this dessert.

Each serving (without coulis) provides

calories 439, total fat 7g, saturated fat 5g, cholesterol 16mg, sodium 118mg, total carbohydrate 85g, dietary fiber 2g, protein 10g

✓✓	calcium
✓	B_1, B_2, B_{12}, D, iron, magnesium, potassium

fast fruit desserts

97

Summer fruit fool

From England comes this old-fashioned delicious dessert. Typically, fruit fools are made by whipping heavy cream, then folding in a purée of cooked fresh fruits. Even though this yogurt version is lower in fat than the traditional one, it's still rich, creamy, and full of flavor — thanks to real whipped cream and ripe berries.

Makes 4 servings

1½ cups fresh blackberries (¾ pint)

1½ cups fresh raspberries (¾ pint)

3 cups ripe strawberries (1½ pints)

2 tablespoons water

⅓ cup sugar

⅔ cup heavy (whipping) cream

1 tablespoon grated orange zest
   (from ½ large orange)

⅔ cup low-fat plain yogurt

To decorate (optional)

Thin strips orange zest

Preparation time: 15 minutes

Cooking time: 8 minutes

Cooling & chilling time: about 2 hours

1 Set aside 1 cup of mixed berries for decorating. In a large heavy saucepan, add the remaining berries and the water. Bring the fruits just to a boil, then reduce the heat and cook gently for 5 minutes or until soft and very juicy. Stir in the sugar and cook 1 minute more or until sugar dissolves.

2 Remove from the heat and let cool slightly, then transfer to a food processor or blender. Process 1 minute or until puréed. Strain into a large bowl, discarding the seeds and pulp. Let cool for 30 minutes; refrigerate until cold.

3 Whip the cream with the grated orange zest until thick. Using a whisk, gently fold in the yogurt, then the cooled fruit purée.

4 Spoon the fool into 4 dessert dishes or goblets. Chill well before serving. Decorate with the reserved berries plus the orange zest, if you wish.

More ideas

• Lemony plum fool: Substitute 6 large ripe plums (about 1 pound) for the berries. Slice 1 unpeeled plum; save for decorating. Peel, pit, and slice the remaining 5 plums, ½ inch thick (you need 4½ cups). Combine these plums with 1½ teaspoons lemon zest and the water and cook 5 minutes or until soft and juicy (step 1).

• Fresh strawberry fool: Buy 2 quarts ripe strawberries (no blackberries or raspberries). Set aside 1 cup of the largest berries for decorating. Thinly slice the rest of the berries into a large bowl, then sprinkle with the ⅓ cup sugar, plus 1 to 2 tablespoons framboise or cassis, if you wish. Let the berries stand at room temperature for 1 hour or until soft and juicy (do not cook). Fold the berries and their juices into the cream-yogurt mixture (step 3).

• Bing cherry fool: Drain two 1-pound cans of pitted Bing cherries. Use in place of the berries (step 1). Cook and strain (step 2). Decorate with the strips of orange zest (step 4).

Each serving provides Ⓥ

calories 312, **total fat** 16g, **saturated fat** 10g, **cholesterol** 57mg, **sodium** 43mg, **total carbohydrate** 41g, **dietary fiber** 7g, **protein** 4g

✓✓✓	C
✓✓	fiber
✓	A, B₂, folate, D, calcium, magnesium, potassium

Healthy tips

• Yogurt is a good source of calcium. Throughout life, but particularly during adolescence and pregnancy, it is important for women to get enough calcium to keep bones healthy and prevent osteoporosis in their later years. Yogurt is also a very good source of vitamin B₂.

• These mixed soft fruits are all rich in the antioxidant vitamin C and an excellent source of fiber. Plus, their natural acidity helps to prevent the loss of this vitamin during cooking. In this strawberry fool, the berries are not cooked.

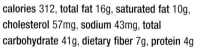

fast fruit desserts

Hot plum sauce

Take a pound of ripe purple plums, then simmer them slowly in fresh orange juice and spices. Strain the plums, sweeten them, and spike them with a little brandy. You'll have a fabulous fresh fruit sauce you can use generously over ice cream, as it has only about one-third the calories of traditional fudge sauce.

Makes 1 cup

1 pound ripe dessert plums

⅔ cup fresh orange juice

1 teaspoon ground cinnamon

⅛ teaspoon ground cloves

1 tablespoon light brown sugar, or to taste

1 tablespoon brandy (optional)

To serve

Scoops of vanilla frozen yogurt, vanilla bean ice cream, or lemon sorbet

Preparation time: 15 minutes

Cooking time: about 10 minutes

1 Cut the plums in half, pit them, and place in a large heavy saucepan. Stir in the orange juice, cinnamon, and cloves. Bring the mixture slowly to a boil, then reduce the heat and simmer gently, uncovered, for 10 minutes or until the fruit is very soft and juicy.

2 In a food processor, process the mixture until smooth, then strain into a medium-size bowl. Add the sugar and stir to mix, then taste the sauce and add more sugar if necessary. Add the brandy, if using.

3 Reheat the sauce if necessary. Serve the sauce hot, drizzled over scoops of frozen yogurt, ice cream, or sorbet.

More ideas

• Fresh blackberry sauce: Substitute 3 cups fresh blackberries for the plums and use ⅔ cup apple juice instead of the orange juice. Simmer blackberries only 5 minutes, not 10 (step 1). Increase light brown sugar to 3 tablespoons (step 2).

• No-cook peach sauce: Instead of the plums, thaw a 20-ounce bag frozen peach slices. Place in a food processor and add the cinnamon and cloves. Strain the purée and sweeten to taste. Serve cold or hot.

• Anytime plum sauce: Substitute a 1-pound can of plums in heavy syrup for the fresh plums. Drain well and add the spices and sugar. Proceed with step 2.

Healthy tips

• Plums provide dietary fiber, including cellulose and pectin. Cellulose, an insoluble fiber, plays a very important role in preventing constipation. Pectin, a soluble fiber, regulates intestinal functions and can help to reduce blood cholesterol levels.

• Vitamin C in this recipe is contributed mainly by the orange juice, though plums do contribute a fair amount, in addition to potassium.

• Eating frozen yogurt or ice cream is a good way of adding calcium to the diet of children and teenagers. As children grow, their need for calcium increases too, especially in their teenage years.

2 tablespoons of sauce provide
calories 48, total fat 0g, saturated fat 0g, cholesterol 0mg, sodium 1mg, total carbohydrate 11g, dietary fiber 1g, protein 1g

✓✓   C

fast fruit desserts

101

Sweet Finales

Fabulous fruit desserts, made the healthy way

YOU CAN STILL FEAST ON YOUR FAVORITE DESSERTS while eating the healthier way. Cutting down on fats and sugars doesn't have to mean you're skipping desserts. Whisk up a queen of a raspberry pudding with a puffy meringue on top, crown poached pears and blueberries with buttery shortbread wedges, or bake a heavenly lemon cheesecake with reduced-fat cheeses. Make a luscious crème brûlée from low-fat milk and fresh rhubarb or a calorie-conscious mousse cake with cocoa and fresh Bing cherries. Freeze the pick of summer berries into a refreshing ice cream, purée them into an icy Italian granita, or swirl them on top of a cheese tart. Then serve with a smile — desserts *can* be as delicious as they are good for you!

Rhubarb and saffron crème brûlée

In French, crème brûlée *literally translates into burnt sugar. Its name comes from a sprinkling of brown sugar on the top of the delicate baked custard. Under a hot broiler, the sugar caramelizes into a brittle topping. Here, a tart compote of fresh rhubarb hides beneath the delicate custard, complementing the rich flavor.*

Makes 6 individual crème brûlées

9 ounces rhubarb, cut into ½-inch dice (1 cup)

¼ cup orange juice

⅓ cup granulated sugar, or to taste

1 cup low-fat milk (2% milkfat)

2 pinches of saffron threads

4 large egg yolks

1 large whole egg

3 tablespoons heavy cream

6 tablespoons packed light brown sugar

Preparation time: 20 minutes
Baking time: 25 minutes
Cooling time: 30 minutes
Chilling time: at least 1 hour

Each crème brûlée provides Ⓥ
calories 228, total fat 8g, saturated fat 4g, cholesterol 191mg, sodium 46mg, total carbohydrate 36g, dietary fiber 1g, protein 5g

✓ A, B₂, B₁₂, C, D, calcium

1 Preheat the oven to 325°F. Put a kettle of water on high heat to boil. Butter six 6-ounce ramekins and place in a shallow baking pan with sides.

2 In a heavy saucepan, bring the rhubarb, orange juice and 3 tablespoons of the granulated sugar to a boil. Reduce the heat to medium-low and cook, uncovered, 5 minutes or until the fruit is just tender and juicy and is still keeping its shape. Let cool.

3 In another heavy saucepan, heat the milk with the remaining granulated sugar and the saffron until bubbles appear round the edge. Meanwhile, using an electric mixer on high, beat the egg yolks, whole egg, and heavy cream until frothy. Reduce the speed to low and slowly blend in the hot sweetened saffron milk to the egg mixture.

4 Divide the rhubarb compote among the 6 ramekin dishes. Tip: To ladle the custard over the fruit, place the base of the ladle on top of the fruit and turn it slowly to ease in the custard. If you pour the custard, it will mix with the rhubarb, forming only one layer, not the two separate layers that are preferred.

5 Pour boiling water into the baking pan until the water comes about two-thirds up the sides of the dishes. Bake the custards for 25 minutes or just until set in the center.

6 Transfer the custards to a rack to cool for 30 minutes. Cover them with plastic wrap and refrigerate for at least 1 hour or until quite cold.

7 Preheat the broiler to high. Evenly sprinkle 1 tablespoon brown sugar on top of each custard. Broil 6 inches from the heat for just a moment or two until the sugar melts and bubbles (watch carefully!). Let custards cool 5 minutes or until a sugary "brittle" forms.

More ideas

• Cranberry crème brûlée: Substitute 6 ounces (1½ cups) fresh cranberries for the rhubarb and 1 teaspoon grated orange zest for the saffron.

• Ruby apple crème brûlée: Instead of rhubarb, use 1 cup diced, peeled cooking apples and ½ cup golden raisins (step 2).

Healthy tips

• Botanically, rhubarb is a vegetable, but it's generally used like a fruit in pies and desserts. Rhubarb rates high in both vitamin C and potassium. Remember, use only the stalks; the leaves are very poisonous.

• Besides providing a high-quality complete protein, eggs are good sources of the fat-soluble vitamin A (needed for proper vision) and vitamin D (for healthy bones).

sweet finales

Pear crêpes with chocolate sauce

Whip up a batch of batter and bake some crêpes...mix up the creamy cheese and fresh pear filling...fill and fold the crêpes. Then simmer up a homemade chocolate sauce to drizzle over all. The sauce has much less fat and sugar than most similar recipes, but it's still a dark rich sauce with a deep chocolate flavor.

Makes 6 servings (2 crêpes each)

Crêpes and almond crème filling

1 cup all-purpose flour

1¼ cups low-fat milk (2% milkfat)

1 large egg

1 tablespoon sunflower oil

8 ounces reduced-fat cream cheese (Neufchâtel)

¼ cup sour cream

¼ cup ground almonds

2 tablespoons granulated sugar

¼ teaspoon pure almond extract

5 large ripe dessert pears, such as Comice

3 tablespoons fresh lemon juice

½ cup sifted confectioners' sugar

Chocolate sauce

5 ounces bittersweet or semisweet chocolate

⅓ cup light corn syrup

2 tablespoons low-fat milk (2% milkfat)

1 tablespoon granulated sugar

½ teaspoon pure vanilla extract

Preparation time: 35 minutes

Standing time: 30 minutes

Cooking time: 20 minutes

Each crêpe provides Ⓥ

calories 313, total fat 13g, saturated fat 7g, cholesterol 37mg, sodium 106mg, total carbohydrate 47g, dietary fiber 4g, protein 6g

✓ B₂, C, copper, fiber

1 First make the batter. Place the flour, milk, egg, and oil in a food processor or blender and process until smooth. Pour the batter into a pitcher and let stand at room temperature for 30 minutes.

2 Heat a 6" crêpe pan or shallow skillet over medium-high heat, then add a few drops of oil. Pour in about 3 tablespoons of the batter and quickly tilt the pan to coat the bottom evenly. Cook until the bottom of the crêpe is brown, then gently turn it over and cook for 15 seconds on the other side. When done, slide the crêpe onto a plate. Repeat, making 12 crêpes in all, sliding each one onto the plate, and separating the crêpes with waxed paper.

3 Preheat the oven to 400°F. To make the filling, put the cream cheese in a small mixing bowl and cream with an electric mixer on medium speed. Blend in the sour cream, almonds, the 2 tablespoons granulated sugar, and the almond extract (do not overmix). Peel, quarter, and core the pears; set aside. Finely chop 3 of the pears; slice the remaining 2 pears ¼ inch thick and sprinkle the pears with the lemon juice.

4 To fill each crêpe, spoon a heaping tablespoon of the cheese filling onto a quarter area of each crêpe and top with a spoonful of chopped pear.

Fold over each crêpe into quarters, to make a triangle, enclosing the filling. Place on a buttered baking pan, sprinkle with the confectioners' sugar, and bake for 8 minutes or until melted.

5 Meanwhile, make the chocolate sauce. In a small saucepan, stir all of the sauce ingredients over medium-low heat until the chocolate melts. Simmer for 5 minutes or until saucy.

6 Serve the crêpes on 6 individual plates and drizzle with the rich chocolate sauce. Arrange the pear slices next to the crêpes and serve.

More ideas

● Raspberry crêpes: Substitute 1 pint (2 cups) fresh raspberries for the pears. Serve with the chocolate sauce or a berry coulis (see page 25), flavored with a little kirsch (cherry brandy).

● Fresh orange crêpes: Peel and section 5 large navel oranges and substitute for the pears.

Healthy tip

● Milk and dairy products are the best source of calcium, which is needed for strong bones and teeth. They are also good sources of protein, important for growth, and of riboflavin (B₂), necessary for a well-functioning nervous system.

sweet finales

Baked almond-stuffed peaches

Turn fresh peaches into a fabulous warm dessert by stuffing them with dried apricots, toasted almonds, and crushed amaretti cookie crumbs, then baking them in the oven until they are brown and bubbly. Another day, try a variation featuring apples instead of peaches and stuffing them with a cinnamon macaroon filling.

Makes 8 servings (half a peach each)

Baked peaches

5 large peaches, ripe but firm
(about 2½ pounds)

Amaretti stuffing

10 ready-to-eat dried apricot halves,
finely chopped

6 packaged amaretti biscuits, crumbled
(½ cup)

2 teaspoons pure almond extract

1 tablespoon brandy

1 large egg white

½ cup chopped blanched almonds

⅓ cup packed light brown sugar

To serve (optional)

Low-fat sour cream or vanilla ice cream

Preparation time: 30 minutes
Cooking time: about 35 minutes

Each serving (half a peach) provides ⓥ

calories 200, total fat 6g, saturated fat 0g, cholesterol 0mg, sodium 5mg, total carbohydrate 34g, dietary fiber 3g, protein 4g

✓ C, magnesium, potassium, copper, fiber

1 Preheat the oven to 350°F. Half-fill a large saucepan with water and bring to a boil over high heat. Cut 4 of the peaches in half (do not peel) and remove the pits. Slide the peaches into the boiling water and cook about 2 minutes or just until they begin to soften. Using a slotted spoon, transfer to paper towels to drain. Place the peaches cut-side up in a shallow baking dish.

2 To make the filling, peel, pit, and finely chop the remaining peach and place in a medium-size bowl. Add the dried apricots, amaretti crumbs, almond extract, brandy, and egg white. Stir until thoroughly mixed.

3 Heat a small, heavy, dry frying pan over high heat for 1 minute, add the almonds, then turn and toss them until golden and lightly toasted. Add the almonds to the fruit mixture and toss.

4 Spoon the filling into the cavities of each peach half, heaping up the filling and pressing it together gently. Sprinkle with the brown sugar. Cover the baking dish with foil.

5 Bake the peaches for 25 minutes or until tender. Remove the foil cover. Increase the oven temperature to 400°F and bake 5 minutes more or until the topping is golden brown. Serve warm with a scoop of sour cream or ice cream, if you wish.

More ideas

• Baked raisin-stuffed apples: Instead of the peaches, substitute 5 large red-skinned baking apples (about 2½ pounds), such as Cortland, Jonathan, Rome Beauty, or York Imperial. Cut 4 of the apples in half (do not peel) and core (step 1). Instead of the amaretti filling, use the remaining peeled, cored, chopped apple, 1 cup coconut macaroon crumbs, ½ cup golden raisins, 1 teaspoon vanilla extract, 1 tablespoon light rum, 1 teaspoon ground cinnamon, and 1 large egg white (step 2).

• Baked cherry-stuffed pears: Substitute 5 large ripe pears for the peaches (step 1) and 1 cup dried cherries for the apricots (step 2).

• Baked cranberry-stuffed nectarines: Use 5 large ripe nectarines for the peaches (step 1) and 1 cup dried cranberries for the apricots. Use ½ cup chopped pistachios for almonds.

Healthy tips

• Peaches and dried apricots provide beta-carotene, which acts as an antioxidant and may protect against certain cancers. Peaches also contain pectin, the soluble fiber that helps lower blood cholesterol.

• Dried apricots are also a good source of potassium, which is needed to maintain normal blood pressure.

• Almonds not only add delicious flavor but also are a good source of vitamin E.

Cherry brandy clafoutis

From the Limousin region of France comes this country-classic dessert. Typically, it's a sweet, light, cake-like batter poured over fruit, usually black cherries, and baked in a flan "case" (dish). Sometimes the fruits are soaked in brandy or fruit liqueur before adding the batter. It's a simple dessert that's simply divine!

Makes 6 individual clafoutis

2 pounds fresh sweet dark Bing cherries, pitted and cut in half (3 cups)

2 to 3 tablespoons brandy

⅔ cup all-purpose flour

½ cup packed light brown sugar

3 large eggs

1 cup low-fat milk (2% milkfat)

1 teaspoon pure vanilla extract

2 tablespoons confectioners' sugar

Preparation time: 30 minutes
Baking time: 20 minutes

Each clafoutis (5 inch) provides Ⓥ

calories 299, total fat 5g, saturated fat 2g, cholesterol 110mg, sodium 60mg, total carbohydrate 57g, dietary fiber 3g, protein 8g

✓ B_1, B_2, B_{12}, C, D, calcium, iron, potassium, copper, fiber

1 Preheat the oven to 400°F. Butter six 10-ounce individual flan dishes (each 5" wide and ¾" high).

2 Divide the cherries equally among the 6 dishes, spreading them out in an even layer. Drizzle the brandy over the cherries. Set aside.

3 In a medium-size bowl, mix the flour and brown sugar. Using an electric mixer on high, beat the eggs until light yellow; beat in the milk and vanilla until frothy. Reduce the speed to low and blend in the flour until a smooth batter forms (do not overmix).

4 Pour the batter slowly over the fruit. Bake the clafoutis for 20 minutes or until lightly golden and set in the center. Dust each clafoutis with confectioners' sugar and serve hot.

More ideas

• Company clafoutis: Place the fruit and batter in a 10" buttered round flan dish, about 1" high. Bake the clafoutis for 25 minutes or until golden and set in the center (step 4).

• Year-round cherry clafoutis: When fresh cherries are not in the market, substitute two 1-pound cans of pitted sweet Bing cherries (step 2). Drain the fruit well and pat dry (you should have about 3 cups of cherries).

• Sugar 'n' spice clafoutis: To the flour-sugar mixture (step 3), mix in ½ teaspoon ground cinnamon and ¼ teaspoon ground nutmeg.

• Fresh peach clafoutis: Instead of the cherries, use 6 ripe large peaches, peeled and sliced (3 cups). For the brandy, substitute 2 tablespoons peach-flavored brandy. To flavor the batter, substitute 1 teaspoon ground pumpkin pie spice for the vanilla, adding the spice to the flour (step 3).

• Red grape clafoutis: Substitute 2 pounds red seedless grapes, for the cherries. Cut each grape in half vertically; you will have about 3 cups (step 2).

Healthy tips

• Cherries not only provide delicious flavor and fiber but also thiamine (vitamin B_1), instrumental in turning carbohydrates, proteins, and fats into energy.

• Substituting skim milk in the batter for the low-fat milk (2% milkfat), you reduce the fat content. At the same time, you get an equal amount of calcium and vitamin D from the milk (calcium is particularly important for maintaining healthy bones).

• Choose grapes: Ounce per ounce, fresh grapes provide three times as much vitamin B_6 and twice as much vitamin B_1 as Bing cherries. Grapes are also good sources of ellagic acid, a phytochemical that helps protect against cancer.

Steamed kumquat honey pudding

Tangy and fruity, kumquats make delicious steamed puddings. If you don't have a steamer, a deep saucepot with a rack and a cover will do just fine. Use a fluted pudding mold, cake pan, or bundt pan with a tube in the center.

Makes 8 servings

Kumquat pudding

2 tablespoons golden honey

1⅔ cups self-rising flour

1 cup packed light brown sugar

⅓ cup fresh fine white breadcrumbs

1 tablespoon baking powder

2 large eggs

½ cup (1 stick) unsalted butter, at room temperature

⅔ cup low-fat milk (2% milkfat)

2 cups fresh kumquats (8 ounces; about 16 kumquats), thinly sliced and seeded

Crème anglaise

1⅔ cups low-fat milk (2% milkfat)

3 large egg yolks

¼ cup granulated sugar

1 teaspoon pure vanilla extract

Preparation time: 30 minutes
Steaming time: 1¾ hours

Each serving provides Ⓥ

calories 451, **total fat** 16g, **saturated fat** 9g, **cholesterol** 169mg, **sodium** 436mg, **total carbohydrate** 69g, **dietary fiber** 3g, **protein** 8g

✓✓	A
✓	B₁, B₂, C, calcium, iron, fiber

1 Butter a 6-cup pudding mold with a center tube and a cover or a 9" bundt or tube cake pan. Drizzle the honey on the bottom and sides.

2 In a large bowl, mix the flour, brown sugar, breadcrumbs, and baking powder. Using an electric mixer on high, beat the eggs until light yellow. Beat in the butter, then the ²/₃ cup milk until thoroughly blended. With a spoon, stir into the flour mixture just until the flour disappears (do not overmix).

3 Bring a teapot of water to a boil. Meanwhile, spoon one-third of the batter in the bottom of the prepared pudding mold. Layer half of the kumquats, then one-third more batter; repeat, ending with batter. Smooth out batter with a spoon. Cover the mold with foil and secure the cover tightly. If using a bundt or tube cake pan, cover it tightly with heavy foil.

4 Place the pudding mold on a rack in the steamer or deep saucepot. Carefully pour in the boiling water from the teapot until the water comes half-way up the sides of the mold. Cover and steam over high heat for 1¾ hours, adding more water when needed.

5 About 20 minutes before serving, make the crème anglaise. In a large heavy saucepan, heat the 1⅔ cups milk until bubbles appear around the edge. Using an electric mixer on high, beat the egg yolks and granulated sugar until light yellow. Beat in about ½ cup of the hot milk, then return to the saucepan. Stir over low heat until the custard lightly coats the back of the spoon. Do not boil. Transfer the custard to a heatproof bowl; stir in the vanilla.

6 When a wooden pick inserted halfway from the edge comes out clean, remove the mold from the steamer. Uncover and discard the foil. Invert the pudding onto a serving plate and shake the pudding gently until it falls onto the plate. Cut with a serrated knife. Serve hot with crème anglaise.

Another idea

• Substitute 2 cups fresh orange sections for the kumquats.

Healthy tips

• Kumquats are not a true citrus fruit, but are closely related. Not surprisingly, they are also an excellent source of vitamin C. Although this vitamin is no longer believed to have a direct effect in preventing the common cold, it does help to maintain the immune system and may decrease the severity and length of infections.

• Milk provides calcium and phosphorus – important for maintaining strong bones and teeth – as well as protein and riboflavin.

sweet finales

Raspberry queen of puddings

In British kitchens, breadcrumbs are often used to give puddings substance and shape. This queen of all puddings is baked in a mold, then crowned with a golden puff of a meringue. The pudding is flavored with cocoa and layered with fresh raspberry purée before the classic meringue finish. A beauty!

Makes 4 individual puddings

3 large eggs

3 tablespoons unsweetened cocoa, sifted

1⅓ cups low-fat milk (2% milkfat)

½ cup sugar

½ cup fresh breadcrumbs

2 tablespoons red currant jelly

1 pint fresh raspberries (2 cups)

¼ cup slivered almonds

Preparation time: 20 minutes
Standing time: 20 minutes
Baking time: 35 minutes

Each pudding provides Ⓥ

calories 329, total fat 10g, saturated fat 3g, cholesterol 166mg, sodium 152mg, total carbohydrate 52g, dietary fiber 4g, protein 11g

✓✓ B₂, C

✓ A, B₁₂, folate, D, calcium, iron, magnesium, potassium, zinc, copper, fiber

1 Butter four 10-ounce soufflé dishes (each 4" wide and 2½" high) and place in a baking pan with enough boiling water to come halfway up the sides of the dishes. Break 1 of the whole eggs into a medium-size bowl. Separate the remaining 2 eggs. Add the yolks to the bowl; set aside the whites.

2 Place the cocoa in a small saucepan, whisk in the milk, and heat just to a boil over medium-high heat. Using an electric mixer on high, beat the egg/egg yolk mixture with 2 tablespoons of the sugar until light yellow. Slowly beat the hot milk into the eggs. Stir in the breadcrumbs.

3 Preheat the oven to 325°F. Divide the batter evenly among the 4 soufflé dishes and let stand for 20 minutes to let the breadcrumbs absorb some of the liquid. Bake for 20 minutes or until set.

4 Meanwhile, melt the red currant jelly over low heat. Add 1¼ cups raspberries, crushing them lightly. Heat gently for 2 minutes, then cool. Layer over the top of the baked puddings.

5 To make meringue, beat egg whites with an electric beater on high until soft peaks form. Add the remaining 6 tablespoons of sugar, beating until glossy. Swirl the meringue into peaks on each pudding. Sprinkle with almonds.

6 Return the puddings to the oven and bake at 325°F for 15 minutes more or until the meringues are puffy and golden brown. Decorate each with a few raspberries and serve immediately.

More ideas

• Fresh apricot queen of puddings: Substitute 1 pound pitted, peeled ripe apricots (2 cups) for the raspberries and 3 tablespoons apricot preserves for the red currant jelly. Chop 1¼ cups of apricots for the puddings (step 4). Use sliced apricots for decorating (step 6).

• Cinnamon 'n' spice queen of puddings: Omit the cocoa powder and flavor the custards with ½ teaspoon ground cinnamon and ¼ teaspoon freshly grated or ground nutmeg.

• For a large pudding, bake in a 1½ quart soufflé dish for 35 minutes or until set (step 3).

Healthy tips

• Raspberries are not only low in calories but also provide plenty of vitamin C. They are high in pectin, which is a soluble fiber that helps control blood cholesterol levels.

• By using cocoa powder instead of baking chocolate in these puddings, you reduce the fat and increase the amount of iron.

• Milk and other dairy products are the best sources of riboflavin (B₂), a vitamin needed to help release energy from foods.

sweet finales

Pear and blueberry shortbread

To make this buttery almond shortbread, just pat out the rich dough onto the baking sheet with your fingers — no rolling is needed. Bake until lightly golden, cut into triangular wedges, and serve on top of warm poached fruits. This way, the shortbread stays crisp and you get to enjoy more fruit than can fit into a typical pie dish.

Makes 6 servings + 12 shortbread wedges

Shortbread pastry

1⅓ cups all-purpose flour
¾ cup (1½ sticks) unsalted butter
⅓ cup sugar
2 tablespoons ground almonds
¼ teaspoon pure almond extract
1 large egg

Poached fruit

5 large ripe dessert pears, such as Anjou, red Bartlett, or green Comice
1¼ cups apple juice
½ pint blueberries (1 cup)

Preparation time: 20 minutes
Baking time: 10 minutes

Each serving + 1 wedge of shortbread provides   (V)

calories 323, total fat 13g, saturated fat 7g, cholesterol 49mg, sodium 10mg, total carbohydrate 52g, dietary fiber 6g, protein 3g

✓ A, B₁, B₂, C, copper, fiber

---

1 Position a rack in the middle of the oven and preheat the oven to 375°F. Line a baking sheet with parchment paper. To make the pastry, put the flour, butter, sugar, ground almonds, and almond extract into a food processor. Process a few seconds to mix. Add the egg and process just until the mixture comes together into a dough, adding a few drops of water if necessary. Or, mix all of the ingredients for the pastry in a bowl by hand with your fingertips.

2 Pat out the dough in the center of the baking sheet to form a circle about 8 inches in diameter and ½ inch high. Pinch the edges to scallop them and lightly score into 12 wedges with the pointed tip of a paring knife. Prick the pastry all over with a fork.

3 Bake the pastry on the middle rack for 10 minutes or until golden. Slide the pastry on the paper to a rack to cool. Cut along the marked lines with a serrated knife, making 12 wedges.

4 While the pastry is baking, peel the pears, cut each one into quarters, and remove the core. Place the pears in a large saucepan, pour in the apple juice, and bring to a boil over high heat. Reduce the heat to medium-low and simmer, uncovered, for 10 minutes or until the pears are almost tender. Add the blueberries and cook 2 minutes more or until the pears turn the rich purple color of the berries.

5 Spoon the poached fruits into 6 individual serving plates with a slotted spoon. Boil the juices in the pan until reduced to ¾ cup. Spoon some over the fruits. Top with shortbread.

More ideas

• Apple and blackberry shortbread: Substitute the almond extract in pastry with ¼ teaspoon ground cinnamon (step 1). Substitute 5 large peeled, cored red cooking apples, such as Jonathan, for the pears and ½ pint (1 cup) fresh blackberries for the blueberries (step 4).

• Nectarine and raspberry shortbread: Substitute 5 large peeled ripe nectarines for the pears and ½ pint (1 cup) fresh raspberries for the blueberries; add ½ teaspoon lemon zest to the juice in the pan.

• Shortbread rounds: Instead of a large circle, cut out small rounds with a 2" fluted cutter.

Healthy tip

• Both eggs and nuts provide protein. Eggs contribute "complete" protein, supplying all of the essential amino acids. Conversely, the protein in nuts (except for peanuts) is "incomplete," as it lacks the important amino acid of lysine. Complement nuts by combining them with a grain, such as flour.

Plum and marzipan pastries

Stuff juicy plums with marzipan, shower them with toasted almonds, and wrap them up in pockets of flaky phyllo pastry. Bake them until golden and crisp and serve with spoonfuls of mock crème fraîche, laced with curaçao.

Serves 4
Plum pastry pockets

5 large ripe dessert plums, such as dark reddish-purple Ace or Queen Ann or black-skinned Friar (about 1½ pounds total)

2 ounces white marzipan, sliced into 4 equal circles

20 phyllo (filo) pastry sheets, thawed if frozen (4 ounces)

6 tablespoons (¾ stick) unsalted butter, melted

¼ cup sliced almonds, toasted

To serve: Mock crème fraîche (optional)

4 ounces reduced-fat cream cheese (Neufchâtel), at room temperature

3 tablespoons low-fat sour cream

2 tablespoons orange marmalade (optional)

1 to 2 tablespoons curaçao (optional)

1 teaspoon confectioners' sugar mixed with ⅟₁₆ teaspoon ground cinnamon

Preparation time: 45 minutes
Cooking time: 15 minutes

Each pastry provides ⓥ

calories 433, total fat 26g, saturated fat 12g, cholesterol 46mg, sodium 143mg, total carbohydrate 49g, dietary fiber 5g, protein 6g

✓✓	C
✓	A, B₁, B₂, niacin, magnesium, potassium, fiber

1 Preheat the oven to 350°F. Cut the plums in half lengthwise (do not peel) and remove the pits. Place a slice of marzipan between the halves of 4 plums and press back together like a sandwich. Cut the remaining plum lengthwise into thin slices and set aside.

2 Cut out 20 phyllo squares, each 10 inches by 10 inches, and quickly cover with plastic wrap, then a damp towel (phyllo dries out in a couple of minutes if left uncovered). Work fast!

3 Place a square of phyllo on a flat work surface and brush very lightly with about a teaspoon of the melted butter. Stack 4 more squares on top, brushing with butter and placing each at a different angle so the corners are off-center. Repeat, making a total of 4 stacks, 5 pastry layers each.

4 For each of the 4 pastry pockets, spoon 1 tablespoon of almonds in the center of a pastry stack and stand a marzipan-stuffed plum on top. Gather the pastry up and around the plum, forming a pouch; twist to close. Brush pastries with the rest of the butter.

5 Place on a nonstick baking tray. Bake for 15 to 20 minutes or until the pastry is crisp and golden. If you wish to serve with the mock crème fraîche, mix the first 4 ingredients and spread on serving plates. Place 1 pastry

pocket on top and circle with the reserved plum slices. Dust with the confectioners' sugar and cinnamon.

More ideas

● Peach pastry pockets: Substitute 5 ripe medium-size peaches for the plums. Peel and pit; cut the peaches in half lengthwise before filling with the marzipan (step 1). Use ¼ cup toasted pecans instead of the almonds (step 4).

● Pear pastry pockets: Substitute 5 ripe medium-size pears for the plums. Peel, core, and cut the pears in half lengthwise before filling with the marzipan (step 1).

● For pastries with a hint of orange, sprinkle the phyllo pastry with the finely grated zest of an orange as you butter and fold the layers, adding only a little zest at a time.

Healthy tips

● The plums in this dessert are a delicious way to help hit the target of at least 5 servings of fruits and vegetables each day.

● Phyllo (filo) pastry, usually made with unsaturated fat and no cholesterol, makes a lower-fat alternative to rich puff pastries. Only very little butter needs to be brushed on the pastry while shaping.

● Almonds and other nuts provide many of the nutrients usually obtained from meat, such as iron and zinc.

Strawberry cheese tart

Bake a very thin, flaky, and crisp tart shell. Spread it with a delicious honey-orange Neufchâtel cheese, instead of a higher-fat pastry cream. Top with an arrangement of fresh berries and drizzle with a sweet currant glaze.

Makes 10 servings

Tart shell
1½ cups all-purpose flour

½ cup (1 stick) unsalted butter, cut into small pieces, at room temperature

3 tablespoons sugar

3 large egg yolks, beaten

Filling
12 ounces reduced-fat cream cheese, (Neufchâtel), at room temperature

2 tablespoons honey

1½ teaspoons grated orange zest

1 tablespoon fresh orange juice

1 quart ripe strawberries, hulled and quartered (about 3 cups)

¾ cup fresh blueberries

¼ cup red currant jelly

Preparation time: 30 minutes

Chilling time: 1½ hours

Baking time: 15 minutes

Each serving provides ⓥ
calories 305, total fat 17g, saturated fat 10g, cholesterol 101mg, sodium 198mg, total carbohydrate 34g, dietary fiber 2g, protein 7g

✓✓✓	C
✓✓	A
✓	B₁, B₂

1 First, make the tart shell. Set out a 9" removable-bottom tart pan. Sift the flour into a medium-size bowl. Make a well in the center and put in the butter, sugar, and beaten egg yolks. With your fingers, work the ingredients in the center together, draw in the flour, and work into a smooth paste. Wrap the pastry dough in plastic wrap, flatten into a 6-inch disk, and chill for 1 hour.

2 On a floured surface, roll out the dough ⅛ inch thick. Shape the shell in the pan and chill for 30 minutes.

3 Preheat the oven to 375°F. Line the tart shell with parchment paper or foil and fill with baking pellets, uncooked rice, or dried beans. "Blind" bake for 10 minutes or until the edges begin to brown. Remove the baking pellets and paper and bake 5 minutes more or until the base of the shell is light golden brown. Cool in the pan on a rack. Carefully remove the pastry rim, leaving the shell on the bottom of the pan, or slide it off onto a cake plate.

4 To make the filling, mix the cheese, honey, orange zest, and juice until smooth. Spread out the filling into the cold shell, pushing it out to the edges.

5 Arrange the strawberries and blueberries over the surface of the filling. Heat the jelly until it is liquid and smooth, then brush generously over the fruit. Chill until set.

More ideas
• Raspberry-peach tart: Make the cheese filling, substituting 2 tablespoons sugar and 1 to 2 teaspoons framboise (raspberry liqueur) for the honey and orange juice (step 4), but do not omit the orange zest. Omit the strawberries and blueberries. Instead, decorate the tart with 4 large ripe, pitted, peeled peaches, cut into slices ¼ inch thick (3 cups) and ½ pint fresh raspberries (1 cup). To glaze, brush the tart with ¼ cup melted apricot jam instead of the red currant jelly.

• Sea Island tart: Mix the filling until smooth (step 4), then stir in ¼ cup flaked coconut. For the fruit, use only 1 cup sliced, hulled strawberries and omit the blueberries (step 5). Add 1 large peeled, seeded papaya, cut into slices ¼ inch thick (2 cups), and 2 peeled kiwis, cut vertically into slices ¼ inch thick. For the glaze, brush with ¼ cup melted guava jelly instead of the red currant jelly (step 5).

Healthy tips
• Strawberries and blueberries are rich sources of vitamin C, which is a vitamin that is believed to help control blood cholesterol.

• Neufchâtel, a reduced-fat cream cheese, has one-third less fat than regular cream cheese.

Black Forest mousse cake

Here's one of those heavenly warm dense chocolate cakes that is very light, surprisingly low in fat, and much easier to make than you might think. Cocoa delivers a rich chocolatey flavor with less fat than plain chocolate.

Makes 6 servings

Mousse cake

½ cup all-purpose flour

½ cup granulated sugar

⅓ cup unsweetened cocoa

⅛ teaspoon salt

5 large egg whites

1 teaspoon pure vanilla extract

1 pound fresh sweet dark Bing cherries, pitted and cut in half (1½ cups)

1 to 2 tablespoons confectioners' sugar

Mock crème fraîche (optional)

4 ounces reduced-fat cream cheese (Neufchâtel), at room temperature

3 tablespoons low-fat sour cream

2 tablespoons cherry conserves

1 to 2 tablespoons kirsch (cherry brandy) or rum (optional)

Preparation time: 20 minutes

Baking time: 25 minutes

1 Preheat the oven to 350°F and line a 9" round cake pan (2" deep) with parchment paper. Sift the flour, ¼ cup of the granulated sugar, the cocoa, and salt on a piece of waxed paper.

2 Using an electric mixer on high, beat the egg whites in a clean, grease-free large bowl until soft peaks form. With the mixer running, beat in the remaining ¼ cup of the granulated sugar, 1 tablespoon at a time, and the vanilla extract. Continue beating until the eggs whites are glossy and smooth, and stand up in stiff peaks.

3 Sift the flour-cocoa mixture over the egg whites and fold in gently with a wire whisk, just until the flour disappears. Do not overmix. Using a rubber spatula, lift the batter into the pan. Smooth out the surface, mounding it slightly in the center, then sprinkle the cherries evenly over the top of the cake.

4 Bake the cake for 25 minutes or until the cake has risen and is just firm to the touch yet still moist on top (a pick inserted into the center should come out with moist crumbs). Transfer the cake to a wire rack to cool slightly.

5 Sprinkle the cake with the confectioners' sugar before serving. If you wish to serve with the mock crème fraîche, blend together all of the ingredients and serve each slice of the warm cake with a generous spoonful.

Healthy tips

• Like egg yolks, egg whites also provide protein but do not contribute any of the fat or cholesterol found in the yolks.

• Ounce per ounce, cocoa contains 79% less fat than baking chocolate and five times as much iron. Your body does not absorb this iron as well as the iron in meat, but the vitamin C in the cherries helps.

More ideas

• Warm strawberry-chocolate mousse cake: In place of the cherries, use 1½ cups sliced ripe strawberries (about 1 pint whole berries).

• Raspberry-chocolate mousse cake: In place of the cherries, buy 1 pint fresh raspberries. Use 1½ cups whole fresh raspberries in the cake (end of step 3) and garnish the warm cake with the rest of the berries.

• Winter black forest mousse cake: When fresh Bing cherries are not in the market, substitute a 1-pound can of pitted, sweet dark cherries (1¾ cups). Drain the cherries well before sprinkling them over the top of the cake batter (step 3).

Each side-dish serving provides Ⓥ

calories 184, total fat 1g, saturated fat 0g, cholesterol 0mg, sodium 94mg, total carbohydrate 41g, dietary fiber 1g, protein 6g

✓ B₂, iron, magnesium, potassium, copper

sweet finales

Sultana lemon cheesecake

Originally from Smyrna, Turkey, comes these small golden-green grapes called sultanas, now primarily used for making light golden raisins. Here, they are soaked in brandy, then baked inside a light creamy cheesecake that's lower in fat than most. Instead of rich sour cream, it's decorated with citrus fruits and glazed with marmalade.

Makes 16 servings

Lemon cheesecake

⅔ cup sultanas (golden raisins)

3 tablespoons brandy

¼ cup ground almonds

4 8-ounce packages reduced-fat cream
   cheese (Neufchâtel), at room temperature

1⅓ cups sugar

¼ cup cornstarch

2 large eggs

1½ teaspoons grated lemon zest

2 teaspoons pure vanilla extract

Citrus topping

2 large navel oranges

2 medium-size white or ruby red grapefruit

¼ cup lemon or orange marmalade

To decorate

Fresh mint leaves

Preparation time: 45 minutes

Baking time: 40 minutes

Cooling & chilling time: about 2½ hours

Each serving provides Ⓥ

calories 266, total fat 12g, saturated fat 6g,
cholesterol 47mg, sodium 329mg, total
carbohydrate 36g, dietary fiber 2g, protein 8g

✓✓	C
✓	A, B₂, calcium

1 Place the sultanas in a small bowl, add the brandy, and let the raisins soak for at least 30 minutes or until most of the brandy has been absorbed.

2 Preheat the oven to 350°F. Butter the bottom and sides of a 8" nonstick springform pan; line the bottom with parchment and butter the paper. Sprinkle the almonds in the pan, tilting the pan to coat both the bottom and sides. Wrap the outside of the pan with foil, covering the bottom and extending halfway up the sides.

3 Using an electric mixer on medium, beat the cream cheese, sugar, and cornstarch in a large bowl for 1 minute. Beat in the eggs, one at a time. Stir in the lemon zest, vanilla, and the sultanas, adding any brandy left in the bowl.

4 Spoon the batter into the prepared pan and smooth the surface. Bake for 40 minutes or until the top of the cake is lightly golden and almost set in the center. Transfer to a rack to cool for 30 minutes. Cover with plastic wrap and chill the cake in the pan for 1 hour.

5 For the topping, peel the oranges and grapefruit with a serrated fruit knife, removing all the white pith. Cut between the membranes, lifting out the sections of fruit. In a small saucepan, melt the marmalade over low heat.

6 Carefully remove the ring from the pan, leaving the cake on the bottom of the pan; place on a serving plate. Brush the top with some of the melted marmalade. Arrange the citrus segments on top in a pinwheel; brush with the rest of the marmalade. Chill the cake for 1 hour more or until the topping is set. Decorate with the fresh mint leaves.

More ideas

• Sour cherry cheesecake: Substitute ⅔ cup chopped, dried pitted cherries for the sultanas.

• Apricot cheesecake: Substitute ⅔ cup chopped dried apricots for the sultanas.

• Berry cheesecake: Omit the sultanas. For the topping, substitute 2 cups sliced, hulled ripe strawberries, 1 cup fresh raspberries, and 1 cup fresh blueberries. Use melted currant jelly instead of marmalade.

Healthy tips

• About 4½ pounds of grapes are needed to make a pound of raisins, making them an excellent concentrated source of nutrients, especially iron, potassium, and fiber. Plus, they are both fat free and cholesterol free.

• The fresh citrus fruit topping provides lots of vitamin C, while not contributing any additional fat.

sweet finales

Summer pudding

What an amazing dish British summer pudding is! It uses fresh peaches and a mix of ripe juicy berries — pick the best your fruit market has to offer. Toss them with sugar to bring out their natural juices, layer them between slices of bread, and let stand overnight. Then slice and enjoy, with spoonfuls of crème fraîche, if you wish.

Serves 6

Fresh fruit pudding

6 cups mixed fresh ripe berries (blackberries, blueberries, raspberries, strawberries)

2 large ripe peaches or nectarines

½ cup sugar

¾ cup cranberry juice, plus ⅓ cup for drizzling

8 thin slices white bread, preferably a day old (about 6 ounces)

To serve: Mock crème fraîche (optional)

4 ounces reduced-fat cream cheese (Neufchâtel), at room temperature

3 tablespoons low-fat sour cream

1 tablespoon crème de cassis

Preparation time: 30 minutes
Standing time: 1 hour
Chilling time: 8 hours or overnight

Each serving (pudding alone) provides Ⓥ

calories 243, total fat 2g, saturated fat 0g, cholesterol 0mg, sodium 151mg, total carbohydrate 56g, dietary fiber 6g, protein 4g

✓✓✓	C
✓	B₁, B₂, niacin, copper, fiber

1 Cut the blackberries in half if they are large; hull and slice the strawberries ¼ inch thick. Peel and pit the peaches, then slice them ¼ inch thick. Combine all the berries and the peaches in a large bowl. Toss the fruits with the sugar and the ¾ cup of cranberry juice. Cover with plastic wrap and let stand at room temperature for about 1 hour or until soft and juicy.

2 Now, prepare the pudding. Butter a 6-cup pudding mold or an 8-inch square baking dish. Using a serrated bread knife, remove the crusts from the bread. Stack the slices into two stacks, 4 slices each. Cut each stack diagonally 2 times, from one corner to the opposite corner, making 32 small bread triangles.

3 Line the bottom of the mold or dish with one-fourth of the bread, then top with one-third of the fruit and their juice. Repeat 2 times, then decorate the top with the remaining bread, pressing down slightly as you work. Drizzle with the remaining ⅓ cup cranberry juice.

4 Cover with plastic wrap. Weight down the pudding with a plate, then a heavy can of food on top. Refrigerate for 8 hours or overnight. To serve, place a serving plate on top of the pudding; invert to unmold. If you wish, blend all of the ingredients together for the mock crème fraîche; serve with the pudding.

More ideas

● Drizzle the fruits with 2 tablespoons cherry brandy, if you wish (step 1).

● Autumn pudding: Instead of the berries and peaches use: 4 cups chopped peeled apples, 3 cups chopped, peeled ripe pears, ⅓ cup dried cranberries, ⅓ cup chopped dried apricots, and ¼ cup golden raisins (step 1). Place in a large saucepan with 1¼ cups apple juice and ½ teaspoon ground cinnamon. Bring to a boil over high heat, reduce heat to medium-low and simmer, uncovered, for 5 minutes or until the apples are tender. Remove from the heat and stir in 2 tablespoons apple brandy. Substitute cinnamon swirl bread for the white bread (step 2). Layer the pudding (step 3), then drizzle with ⅓ cup of apple juice.

Healthy tips

● Strawberries are an excellent source of vitamin C; blackberries and raspberries, a good source; blueberries, a fair source. This vitamin is not only an antioxidant which may help in preventing heart disease, but it is also essential for healing wounds and resisting infections.

● Since this pudding is low in fat and high in carbohydrates, it's the perfect dessert to include in a heart-healthy diet.

large eggs > 6
Apple-carmel
sauce

any berry

...me caramel

...ade with a sugar-based caramel and a rich creamy custard. This fruity version
...amel and the custard, to reduce the fat and sugar content. The dessert is a lighter,
...ul departure from tradition — but still delicious!

Custard
3 large eggs
3 large egg yolks
⅓ cup sugar
2 cups apple juice

To serve
1 pint fresh blackberries (2 cups)

Preparation time: 35 minutes
Baking time: 35 minutes
Cooling & chilling time: at least 2½ hours

Each custard provides 🅥
calories 222, **total fat** 5g, **saturated fat** 2g,
cholesterol 213mg, **sodium** 40mg, **total**
carbohydrate 39g, **dietary fiber** 3g, **protein** 5g

✓   A, B₂, C, potassium, fiber

1 Preheat the oven to 325°F.
Set out 6 ovenproof ramekins
(5 or 6 ounces each).

2 To make the caramel, pour the
apple juice into a large, heavy,
nonaluminum saucepan; add the
cinnamon. Bring to a boil over high
heat, then continue boiling, uncovered,
for 20 minutes or until the juice is
reduced by half. Reduce the heat to
medium and boil 10 minutes more or
until the bubbling mixture is reduced to
a golden-brown syrup. Watch carefully,
as it can burn very easily at this stage.

3 Divide the syrup among the
6 ramekins, swirling and spreading
the caramel up the sides of the dishes.
It may not swirl as easily as ordinary
caramel, but do not worry.

4 For the custard, use an electric
mixer set on high to beat the eggs,
egg yolks, and sugar until thickened.
Heat the apple juice in a saucepan until
it comes to a boil. While still beating,
slowly drizzle the hot juice into the egg
mixture until blended. Pour the custard
into the 6 caramel-lined ramekins.

5 Set the ramekins in a baking pan
with sides. Pour enough hot water
into the pan to come halfway up the
sides of the ramekins. Bake custards for
35 minutes or until set in the centers.
Cool 30 minutes; chill at least 2 hours.

6 To serve, loosen each cold custard
from its ramekin by running a knife
around the edge. Turn out each custard
onto a dessert plate so it "floats" in a
pool of the apple-caramel sauce.
Surround with fresh blackberries.

Another idea
• Spanish orange custards (*Flans de naranjas*):
For a lovely, light orange custard, do not make
the caramel. Prepare the custard by substituting
2½ cups fresh orange juice (from about
2½ pounds of oranges) for the apple juice. Heat
the orange juice with 1½ teaspoons orange
zest, and slowly beat into the egg and sugar
mixture (step 4). Pour into 6 molds and bake as
directed. Unmold onto individual dessert plates
and serve with fresh orange sections — a
mixture of ordinary and blood oranges is
stunning. The raw oranges are packed with
vitamin C.

Healthy tips
• Apple juice provides good amounts of
potassium. It works along with sodium to
regulate the body's fluid balance, proper
muscle function, stable blood pressure, and
a healthy heart.
• Blackberries are unique, as they are high
in fiber, as well as vitamin C.

sweet finales

128

Frozen raspberry yogurt

Thanks to the ice-cream machines available today, homemade frozen desserts, such as this one, are almost as easy as turning on a switch. This fresh-made dessert has less sugar than store-bought frozen yogurt.

Makes 1 quart

1 quart fresh raspberries (4 cups)
¼ cup seedless raspberry jam
2 tablespoons bottled rosewater
2 tablespoons crème de cassis (optional)
2 cups plain low-fat yogurt (1 pound)
⅓ cup confectioners' sugar

To decorate (optional)

Fresh raspberries (about 1 cup)
Fresh mint leaves

Preparation time: 20 minutes
Freezing time: about 3 hours if using an
   automatic ice cream machine; 4 hours in
   the freezer

Each serving (½ cup scoop) provides Ⓥ
calories 110, total fat 1g, saturated fat 0.5g,
cholesterol 4mg, sodium 41mg, total
carbohydrate 22g, dietary fiber 3g, protein 4g

✓✓	C
✓	B₂, calcium, fiber

1 Put the raspberries into a large heavy saucepan, then stir in the jam. Cook the mixture over low heat, stirring occasionally, for 5 minutes or until the berries are soft and puréed.

2 Strain the raspberry mixture into a large bowl, discarding the seeds. Stir in the rosewater and the crème de cassis, if you wish. Whisk in the yogurt and the sugar until thoroughly blended.

3 Pour the fruit mixture into an ice-cream machine and freeze, according to the manufacturer's instructions, until the mixture is frozen, smooth, and creamy. Spoon into a large freezerproof container and place in the freezer for at least 2 hours.

4 If you do not have an ice-cream machine, pour the mixture into a large freezerproof container and freeze for 1 hour or until frozen around the edges. Transfer the mixture to a large bowl and beat with an electric mixer or a whisk until smooth. Return to the freezer for 30 minutes more, then beat again. Repeat freezing and beating until the frozen yogurt is smooth and free of ice crystals; freeze at least 2 hours more. If the yogurt has been in the freezer longer than 1 hour, transfer to the refrigerator to soften for about 20 minutes before serving. Decorate with the raspberries and mint leaves, if you wish.

Healthy tips

• Yogurt is an excellent source of calcium, which builds strong teeth and bones and is vital to proper muscle and nerve functions. It is also an excellent source of phosphorus, which helps maintain strong teeth and bones and is essential for proper metabolism.
• Raspberries are an excellent source of vitamin C, which helps control blood cholesterol levels and helps prevent atherosclerosis. Vitamin C also strengthens blood vessel walls, promotes the healing of wounds, and helps the body absorb iron.

More ideas

• Frozen peach yogurt: Substitute 4 cups frozen peach slices (1¼ pounds) for the fresh raspberries. Instead of cooking the fruit, place the peaches and ¼ cup granulated sugar in a food processor or blender and process until smooth. Add the 2 cups plain low-fat yogurt and 2 tablespoons Cointreau (orange liqueur) and process 30 seconds more until blended. Freeze and serve (steps 3 and 4).
• Frozen blackberry yogurt: Substitute 4 cups fresh blackberries for the raspberries (step 1).
• Frozen strawberry yogurt: Substitute 4 cups ripe strawberries for the raspberries (step 1).

Tropical trifle

Originating in England, trifles are popular ways to turn leftover cake or ladyfingers into a spectacular dessert. Here it's bursting with exotic fruits, such as mangoes, bananas, and papayas. A grand way to end dinner!

Makes 6 servings

½ 8-inch angel food or sponge cake

1 large lime

1 large juice orange

3 tablespoons sherry or Madeira

1 small ripe mango, peeled and pitted

2 large bananas

1 large papaya, peeled and seeded

⅔ cup heavy (whipping) cream

3 tablespoons sugar

½ cup low-fat vanilla yogurt

Custard

2 cups low-fat milk (2% milkfat)

3 large egg yolks

2 tablespoons all-purpose flour

2 tablespoons sugar

To decorate

½ cup flaked coconut, toasted

2 star fruits, sliced

Preparation time: 1 hour

Chilling time: at least 4 hours or overnight

Each serving provides Ⓥ

calories 461, total fat 18g, saturated fat 11g, cholesterol 150mg, sodium 281mg, total carbohydrate 69g, dietary fiber 4g, protein 9g

✓✓✓	C
✓✓	A, B₂, B₆
✓	B₁, B₁₂, folate, D, calcium, magnesium, potassium, copper, fiber

1 Tear the cake into bite-size pieces and place in a 3-quart clear-glass serving bowl. Remove the zest from the lime and orange; finely chop and set aside. In a cup, mix the lime and orange juices and the sherry, then sprinkle over the cake. In a food processor, purée the mango; spoon over the cake. Toss to coat well; set aside.

2 Now, make the custard. In a medium-size saucepan, combine the milk and 1 tablespoon of the mixed lime and orange zests; bring to a boil over medium-high heat. While the milk heats, using an electric mixer on high, beat the egg yolks, flour, and sugar in a medium-size bowl until light yellow and smooth. Beat some of the hot milk into the egg mixture, then return to the saucepan. Stir and cook over low heat for 7 minutes or until the custard thickens (do not boil). Remove from the heat and cool until lukewarm.

3 Slice the bananas and papaya ¼ inch thick and arrange on top of the mango layer. Pour the custard evenly over the fruit; cover with plastic wrap and refrigerate until cold and set, about 4 hours or preferably overnight.

4 Using an electric mixer on high, whip the cream until frothy. Add the sugar and continue beating until stiff peaks form. Fold in the yogurt and swirl into peaks on top of the trifle. Sprinkle the trifle with the toasted coconut; decorate with slices of the star fruits.

More ideas

● Strawberry trifle: Omit the lime zest and juice. Use the zest and juice of 2 large oranges instead of only 1. Substitute 3 tablespoons raspberry liqueur (framboise) for the sherry (steps 1 and 2). Use 3 cups of sliced fresh strawberries instead of a papaya (step 3).

● Peach trifle: Substitute 3 tablespoons orange liqueur, such as Grand Marnier, for the sherry (step 1). Substitute 3 cups peeled, ripe peach slices for the papaya (step 3).

● Raspberry trifle: Use 1 cup raspberry purée for the mango purée (step 1). Substitute 3 cups fresh raspberries for the papaya (step 3).

Healthy tips

● The bananas in this recipe are a fair source of potassium, which is important in maintaining blood pressure and is needed for muscle contraction. Another heart-healthy nutrient is vitamin C, which is found in citrus fruits and papaya.

● Mangoes are an excellent source of beta-carotene, which the body converts into vitamin A. This vitamin is essential for healthy skin and good vision. Beta-carotene is also now recognized as an antioxidant nutrient which may reduce the risk of certain cancers, such as lung cancer.

Strawberry and cranberry granita

From Italy with love, flavor, and beauty. Granita is an Italian ice that's made of very fine-grained frozen crystals. This one begins with a purée of fresh ripe strawberries and cranberry juice. The secret to its velvety, almost fluffy texture is stirring the mixture as it freezes, breaking up the ice into tiny crystals that burst with flavor.

Makes 1½ pints (4 servings)

1 quart ripe strawberries, hulled and
    sliced (3 cups)
½ cup sugar
1 cup cranberry juice

To decorate (optional)

12 whole ripe strawberries
12 whole ripe raspberries

Preparation time: 15 minutes
Standing time: 30 minutes
Freezing time: at least 2 hours

Each serving provides Ⓥ
calories 177, total fat 1g, saturated fat 0g,
cholesterol 0mg, sodium 4mg, total
carbohydrate 45g, dietary fiber 3g, protein 1g

✓✓✓	C
✓	fiber

1 Put the strawberries in a large bowl, sprinkle over the sugar, and toss to mix. Cover with plastic wrap and let the berries stand at room temperature for 30 minutes to pull out the juices.

2 Place strawberries and any juices that have collected in the bowl in a food processor or blender and process to a smooth purée. Set aside ⅓ cup of the purée to serve as a sauce.

3 Pour the cranberry juice into the remaining purée and process a few seconds to blend. Pour this mixture into a shallow metal tray. Freeze for about 30 minutes or until the mixture appears to be softly set around the edges.

4 Using a fork, scrape the partially frozen crystals from the edge of the tray into the unfrozen fruit mixture in the center. Return the tray to the freezer and freeze 20 minutes more. Scrape the frozen crystals into the center again, then return to the freezer once more. Repeat this scraping and freezing two or three more times, until you have a mixture that consists of separate, almost fluffy, soft tiny ice crystals.

5 Serve the granita in 4 dessert goblets, footed sherbets, or bowls. Decorate with the whole strawberries and raspberries, if you wish. Spoon some of the reserved berry purée over each serving.

More ideas

- Raspberry-strawberry granita: Use 2 cups sliced strawberries and 1 cup raspberries.
- Blackberry granita: Substitute 1 quart fresh blackberries for the strawberries. Strain the berry-cranberry mixture before pouring it into the ice cube trays (step 3).
- Fresh orange granita: Substitute 3 cups fresh orange slices for the strawberries and 1 cup fresh orange juice for the cranberry juice.
- Fruit sorbet: Turn any of these granitas into a sorbet by freezing the purée mixture in a divided ice cube tray until hard (step 3). Pop the cubes out of the tray and whirl in a processor with about 6 tablespoons juice used in the recipe until light and fluffy. Serve immediately.
- Easy-does-it sorbet: Whirl the mixture into a sorbet in an ice cream machine, following the manufacturer's instructions.

Healthy tips

- Strawberries are an excellent source of vitamin C, contributing more of this vitamin than any other berry. They are also low in calories and high in pectin and other soluble fibers that help reduce cholesterol in the body.
- Cranberry juice contains a natural antibiotic substance that prevents E-coli bacteria from attaching to the bladder walls, guarding against urinary-tract infections.

sweet finales

Persian almond crème

These iridescent molded crèmes, delicately perfumed with almond, are set off to perfection by the exotic flavors and beautiful colors of the fresh fruits. Very little sugar is needed, as the fruit provides natural sweetness.

Makes 4 molded desserts

Molded almond crème

2 cups low-fat milk (2% milkfat)

2 teaspoons powdered unflavored gelatin (1 envelope)

¼ cup sugar

1 teaspoon pure almond extract

Fruit salad

1 large juice orange, such as Hamlin or Jaffa (about 6 ounces)

⅔ cup water

3 tablespoons sugar

2 cardamom pods, very lightly crushed, or ¼ teaspoon ground cardamom

1 tablespoon fresh lemon juice

1 tablespoon orange-flower water or ¼ teaspoon orange extract

2 large navel oranges (about 1 pound)

2 large bananas

½ pomegranate

Preparation time: 30 minutes

Chilling time: at least 2 hours

Each dessert provides

calories 309, total fat 3g, saturated fat 2g, cholesterol 9mg, sodium 66mg, total carbohydrate 67g, dietary fiber 5g, protein 8g

✓✓✓	C
✓✓	B₆
✓	A, B₁, B₂, folate, D, calcium, magnesium, potassium, fiber

1 Oil 4 individual decorative dessert molds (5 or 6 ounces each). Pour ⅔ cup of the milk into a small saucepan and sprinkle over the gelatin. Let stand, without stirring, for 5 minutes or until softened.

2 Add the ¼ cup sugar. Stir over low heat until the gelatin and sugar completely dissolve (do not let boil). Remove from the heat and whisk in the remaining 1⅓ cups milk and the almond extract. Pour into the dessert molds, filling them almost to the top. Cover the molds with plastic wrap; refrigerate at least 2 hours or until set in the centers.

3 Meanwhile, using a citrus zester, remove the zest from the juice orange in long thin strips. Squeeze the juice into a saucepan (you need ½ cup of juice). Stir in the zest, water, sugar, and cardamom pods. Stir over medium-high heat until the mixture comes to a boil and the sugar dissolves. Boil 7 minutes more or until the mixture is reduced and syrupy. Remove from the heat, stir in the lemon juice and orange-flower water, and cool.

4 Peel and section the navel oranges. Cut crosswise into round slices. Peel and slice the bananas. Scoop out the seeds from the pomegranate half. Toss the fruit with the syrup in a bowl.

5 Turn out the molds onto individual plates. Spoon over the fruits.

Healthy tip

● Gelled milk desserts, often called milk jellies, were popular with the Victorians. The nannies recognized that the calcium in milk is particularly important for growing children to build strong bones. So these jellies were often served in the nursery.

Another idea

● Berry-red wine jelly: Substitute 2 cups cranberry juice and ⅔ cup fruity red wine (either alcoholic or nonalcoholic) for the milk. Purée ½ pint (1 cup) each fresh blackberries and blueberries, then press through a sieve to remove the seeds. Whisk the berry purée with the cranberry juice and wine and blend in ¼ teaspoon ground nutmeg. Increase the unflavored gelatin to 4 teaspoons (2 envelopes) and increase sugar to ⅓ cup. Soften and dissolve the gelatin as directed (steps 1 and 2). Omit the almond extract. Oil a 6-cup decorative dessert mold, pour in the berry mixture, and chill for 3 hours or until set in the center. In the fruit salad, substitute ½ pint (1 cup) fresh blackberries and ½ pint (1 cup) fresh raspberries for the bananas (step 4).

sweet finales

Sweet balsamic berry ice cream

Save summer's bounty of fresh berries by swirling and freezing them into this luscious ice cream. Start with the ripest, juiciest berries you can find. Whirl them into this reduced-fat ice cream, which is made with a light sugar syrup instead of a higher-fat rich egg custard. Sparkle up the flavor with a splash of balsamic vinegar.

Makes 1 quart

Berry ice cream

1 quart ripe strawberries, hulled (4 cups)
1 pint fresh raspberries (2 cups)
1½ cups fresh blueberries
2 teaspoons balsamic vinegar
1 cup sugar
⅔ cup water
⅔ cup heavy (whipping) cream

Fresh strawberry compote

1 quart ripe strawberries, hulled (4 cups)
2 tablespoons sugar
Splash of balsamic vinegar
Dash of freshly ground black pepper

To decorate

Fresh mint leaves

Preparation time: 45 minutes
Chilling time: 1 hour
Freezing time: about 3 hours if using an
    automatic ice-cream machine; 4 hours in
    the freezer

Each serving (½ cup scoop) provides Ⓥ
calories 243, total fat 8g, saturated fat 5g,
cholesterol 27mg, sodium 11mg, total
carbohydrate 44g, dietary fiber 4g, protein 2g

✓✓✓	C
✓	fiber

1 Place 1 quart of the strawberries, the raspberries, and blueberries in a food processor or blender and process until smooth. Strain into a large bowl and stir in the 2 teaspoons balsamic vinegar. Refrigerate for 30 minutes.

2 While the berries chill, stir the sugar and water in a small saucepan over high heat until the sugar dissolves. Without stirring, bring the mixture to a boil and continue to boil, uncovered, for 5 minutes or until a light syrup forms. Pour the syrup into a heatproof bowl and let cool for 15 minutes. Stir in the puréed berries; refrigerate for 1 hour.

3 In a small bowl with an electric mixer on high, whip the cream until stiff peaks form, then fold into the cold berry mixture. Pour into an ice-cream machine and freeze, according to the manufacturer's instructions. Spoon the mixture into a freezerproof container; place in the freezer for at least 2 hours.

4 If you do not have an ice-cream machine, pour the mixture into a large freezerproof container, cover with plastic wrap, and freeze for 1 hour or until frozen around the edges. Transfer the mixture to a large bowl and beat with an electric mixer or a whisk until smooth. Return to the freezer for 30 minutes more, then beat again. Repeat freezing and beating until the ice cream is smooth and free of ice crystals; freeze at least 2 hours more.

5 To make the strawberry compote, slice the other quart of strawberries into a serving bowl. Sprinkle with the sugar, then add the splash of balsamic vinegar and a little freshly ground black pepper. Stir, then chill until ready to serve.

6 Transfer the ice cream to the refrigerator for about 20 minutes or until soft enough to scoop. Serve with the strawberry compote; decorate with sprigs of mint.

Another idea

● Fresh peach ice cream: Substitute 8 cups peeled ripe peach slices (about 3 pounds) for the berries (step 1). Serve with a raspberry compote instead of strawberries.

Healthy tip

● Strawberries, raspberries, and blueberries make this dessert an excellent source of vitamin C, which plays a vital role in repairing damaged tissues and in healing wounds. Vitamin C also helps maintain the immune system. It is a powerful antioxidant that protects iron from oxidizing and thus enhances iron absorption.

A glossary of nutritional terms

Antioxidant These are compounds that help to protect the body's cells against the damaging effects of free radicals. Vitamins C and E, beta-carotene (the plant form of vitamin A), and the mineral selenium, together with many of the phytochemicals found in fruit and vegetables, all act as antioxidants.

Calorie A unit used to measure the energy value of food and the intake and use of energy by the body. The scientific definition of 1 calorie is the amount of heat required to raise the temperature of 1 gram of water by 1 degree centigrade. The term kilocalories (abbreviated to *kcal*) is equivalent to 1,000 calories. A person's energy (calorie) requirement varies based on his or her age, sex, and level of activity. *(See also Pyramid, pages 6 and 7.)*

Carbohydrates These substances provide about half of the energy needs for the body. Carbohydrates are divided into two groups: simple carbohydrates, or sugars; and the complex carbohydrates, or starches and fibers. The sugars come mainly from foods of plant origin except for lactose, which comes from milk and milk products.

Sugars are digested and absorbed rapidly to provide energy very quickly. Fructose, the sweetest of sugars, occurs naturally in fruits and honey.

Complex carbohydrates are long chains of the simple sugar called glucose. Plant cells store glucose as starches just as the body stores glucose as glycogen. All starchy foods come from plants. Starches are digested more slowly than sugars. The best food sources include grains and grain products, such as bread, cereals, corn, pasta, potatoes, rice, and other starchy vegetables (sweet potatoes and parsnips).

Fibers are the structural parts of plants that are not digested by the human digestive enzymes. *(See also Fiber, this page, 140, middle column.)*

Daily Values

Total Fat	65 grams
Saturated Fat	20 grams
Cholesterol	300 mg
Sodium	2,400 mg
Carbohydrate	300 grams
Dietary Fiber	25 grams
Protein	50 grams
Vitamin A	5,000 IU or 1,500 μg RE
Vitamin B$_1$ (thiamin)	1.5 mg
Vitamin B$_2$ (riboflavin)	1.7 mg
Niacin (Niacin Equivalent/NE)	20 mg
Vitamin B$_6$	2 mg
Vitamin B$_{12}$	6 μg
Folate	400 μg
Vitamin C	60 mg
Vitamin D	400 IU or 10 μg
Vitamin E	30 IU or 9 mg α-TE
Calcium	1,000 mg
Iron	18 mg
Magnesium	400 mg
Potassium	3,500 mg
Zinc	15 mg
Copper	2 mg

Cholesterol An integral part of cell membranes, cholesterol is a waxy substance that is important to many body compounds such as bile, acids, sex hormones, adrenal hormones, and vitamin D. Cholesterol made by the body is called blood cholesterol. Cholesterol, found only in foods of animal origin, is referred to as dietary cholesterol. High blood cholesterol levels are an important risk factor for coronary heart disease, but the liver makes most of the cholesterol in our blood—only 25% comes from cholesterol in food. So the best way to reduce blood cholesterol is to eat less saturated fat and to increase your intake of foods containing soluble fiber. Recommended intake level is 300 milligrams daily.

Daily Values (DV) Frequently appearing on food labels, Daily Values are standard values of nutrients for adults and children over 4 years old. Developed by the Food and Drug Administration (FDA), they are based on the Recommended Dietary Allowances (RDA). They also include information on other food components, such as fat and fiber.

Dietary Guidelines for Americans (1995) Healthy eating guidelines that were developed for healthy people over the age of two years by the U.S. Department of Agriculture (USDA) and the U.S. Department of Health and Human Services. *(For Guidelines, see page 6.)*

Fat Although a small amount of fat is essential for good health, many people consume far too much. Healthy eating guidelines recommend that no more than 30% of our daily energy intake (calories), or 65 grams per a 2,000 calorie diet, should come from fat. Each gram of fat contains 9 kcal, more than twice as many calories as carbohydrates or protein.

Fats can be divided into three main groups: saturated, monounsaturated, and polyunsaturated. *Saturated fatty acids* are found mainly in animal fats, such as butter and other dairy products and in fatty meat. A high intake of saturated fat is known to be a risk factor for coronary heart disease and certain types of cancer. Current guidelines are that no more than 10% of our daily calories should come from saturated fats, which is about 20 grams in a 2,000 calorie diet.

Where saturated fats tend to be solid at room temperature, the *unsaturated fatty acids*—monounsaturated and polyunsaturated—tend to be liquid. *Monounsaturated fats* are found predominantly in olive oil, peanut oil, rapeseed oil, and avocados. Foods high in *polyunsaturates* include most vegetable oils; the exceptions are saturated palm oil and coconut oil.

The body can make both saturated and monounsaturated fatty acids, but certain polyunsaturated fatty acids, known as *essential fatty acids*, must be supplied by food. There are two "families" of these fatty acids: *omega-6*, derived from linoleic acid, and *omega-3*, from linolenic acid. The main food sources of the *omega-6* family are vegetable oils (such as corn, safflower, soybean), and sunflower seeds, nuts, and leafy vegetables. *Omega-3* fatty acids are provided by oily fish, nuts, and vegetable oils, such as soybean and canola.

Fiber Technically non-starch polysaccharides (NSP), fiber is the term commonly used to describe several different compounds, such as pectin, hemicellulose, lignin, and gums, which are found in the cell walls of all plants. The body cannot digest fiber, but it plays an important role in helping us stay healthy.

Fiber can be divided into two groups: soluble and insoluble. Most plant foods provide both, but some foods are particularly good sources of one type or the other. *Soluble fiber* (in apples and citrus fruits, barley, legumes, and oats) can help reduce high blood cholesterol levels and control blood sugar levels by slowing down the absorption of sugar. *Insoluble fiber* (in cereals, corn bran, wheat bran, whole-grain breads, and vegetables) speeds the passage of waste material though the body. In this way it helps to prevent constipation, hemorrhoids, and diverticular disease; it may also protect against bowel cancer.

Recommended guidelines suggest eating 25 grams or more of fiber daily (about two times the current intake levels in the U.S.).

Food Guide Pyramid This guide is an outline of what to eat daily to help follow the Dietary Guidelines for Americans. The Pyramid is based on the U.S. Department of Agriculture's research on what Americans eat, what nutrients are in these foods, and how to make the best food choices. *(See also Pyramid, pages 6 and 7.)*

Free radicals These highly reactive molecules can cause damage to cell walls and DNA (the genetic material found within cells). They are believed to be involved in the development of heart disease, some cancers, and premature aging. The body naturally produces free radicals; but certain factors, such as cigarette smoke, pollution, and overexposure to sunlight, can accelerate their production.

Glycemic Index (GI) This is used to measure the rate that carbohydrate foods are digested and converted into sugar (glucose and glycogen) to raise blood sugar levels and provide energy. Foods with a high GI are quickly broken down and offer an immediate energy boost; those with a lower GI are absorbed more slowly, making you feel full longer and helping to keep blood sugar levels constant. High-GI foods include table sugar, honey, and watermelon. Low-GI foods include dried apricots, cherries, grapefruit, pears, whole-grain cereals, oats, and pasta. *(See also Fruit and fiber — the GI factor, page 23.)*

Minerals These inorganic substances perform a wide range of vital functions. The *macrominerals* — calcium, chloride, magnesium, potassium, sodium, and sulfur — are present and needed in the largest amounts by the body. Trace minerals, or *microminerals,* are present in the body in amounts less than 5 grams and include chromium, copper, iron, selenium, and zinc.

There are important differences in the body's ability to absorb minerals from different foods, which can be affected by the presence of other substances. For example, oxalic acid, present in spinach, interferes with the absorption of much of the iron and calcium that spinach contains.
• *Calcium* is essential for the development of strong bones and teeth. It also plays an important role in blood clotting. Good sources include dairy products,

glossary

canned fish (eaten with their bones), and dark green leafy vegetables.

• **Chloride** helps to maintain the body's fluid balance. The main source in the diet is table salt.

• **Chromium** is important in the regulation of blood sugar levels. Good dietary sources include unrefined foods, especially liver, brewer's yeast, whole grains, nuts, and cheeses.

• **Copper**, a component of many enzymes, is needed for bone growth and the formation of connective tissue. It helps the body absorb iron from food. Good sources include seafood, nuts, grains, seeds and legumes.

• **Iron** is an essential component of hemoglobin, the pigment in red blood cells that carries oxygen around the body. Good sources include eggs, fish, legumes, meats, nuts, poultry, whole grain and enriched breads and cereals, and some dried fruits such as dried apricots.

• **Magnesium** is important for healthy bones, the release of energy from food, and nerve and muscle function. Good sources include chocolate, cocoa, dark green leafy vegetables, legumes, nuts, seafood, and whole grains.

• **Potassium**, along with sodium, is important in maintaining the balance of fluid in the body and regulating blood pressure. It is also essential for the transmission of nerve impulses. Good sources include fruit, especially bananas and citrus fruits, legumes, nuts, potatoes, and seeds.

• **Selenium** is a powerful antioxidant that protects cells against damage by free radicals. Good sources include grains, meats, and seafood.

• **Sodium** works with potassium to regulate fluid balance, and is essential for nerve and muscle function. Only a little sodium is needed; we tend to get too much in our diet. The main source in the diet is table salt, as well as salty processed foods and ready-prepared foods.

• **Sulfur** is a part of the essential amino acid methionine, as well as two B vitamins, thiamin and biotin. All protein-containing foods, such as eggs, fish, legumes, meats, milk, nuts, and poultry, are good sources.

• **Zinc** is part of many enzymes and is associated with insulin. It is also involved in the transport of vitamin A and in taste perception. Good sources include protein-containing foods, such as eggs, liver, meat, seafood (especially oysters), as well as whole-grain cereals.

Phytochemicals Found in most plant foods, these biologically active compounds are believed to be beneficial in disease prevention. Among the literally thousands, here are a few:

• **Allicin**, a phytochemical found in garlic, onions, leeks, chives, and shallots, is believed to help lower high blood cholesterol levels and stimulate the immune system.

• **Bioflavonoids** are compounds that provide the yellow and orange colors in fruits and vegetables. They act as antioxidants and are believed to reduce the risk of cancer and heart disease. Three of the more popular bioflavonoids include *quercetin*, *rutin*, and *hesperidin*. Some of the best food sources include apricots, blackberries, dark cherries, plums, and rose hips.

• **Carotenoids**, the best known of which are *beta-carotene* and *lycopene*, are powerful antioxidants thought to help protect us against certain types of cancer. Highly colored fruits and vegetables are excellent sources of carotenoids, such as black currants, carrots, mangoes, sweet potatoes, pumpkin, tomatoes, and dark green leafy vegetables.

• **Glucosinolates**, found mainly in cruciferous vegetables, particularly broccoli, Brussels sprouts, cabbage, cauliflower, and kale, are believed to have strong anti-cancer effects. *Sulforaphane* is one of the powerful cancer-fighting substances produced by glucosinolates.

• **Phytoestrogens** have a chemical structure similar to the female hormone estrogen. They are believed to help protect against hormone-related cancers, such as breast and prostate cancer. One type of phytochemical, called *isoflavone*, may help to relieve symptoms associated with menopause. Soybeans are a particularly rich source of isoflavones.

Protein This nutrient is necessary for growth and development, for maintenance and repair of cells, and for the production of enzymes, antibodies, and hormones. It is essential to keep the body working efficiently. Protein is made up of *amino acids*, compounds which contain the four elements necessary for life: carbon, hydrogen, oxygen, and nitrogen. We need all twenty amino acids commonly found in plant and animal proteins. The human body can make eleven, but the remaining nine—called *essential amino acids*—must be obtained from food.

Protein comes in a wide variety of foods. Dairy products, eggs, fish, meat, and soybeans contain all of the essential amino acids, and are called *complete proteins*. Cereals, legumes, nuts, and seeds are also good sources of protein, but they lack one or more of the essential amino acids, so they are referred to as *incomplete proteins*. If you include a variety of protein foods in your diet, both from animal and plant sources, your body will get all the amino acids it needs. It is important to eat protein foods every day, because the body cannot store essential amino acids for later use. The recommended intake level is 50 grams in a 2,000 calorie diet.

Vitamins Organic compounds essential for good health, vitamins are required in only small amounts. Each vitamin performs specific vital functions. Since the human body cannot make most vitamins, they must be obtained from the diet. The body is capable of storing some vitamins (A, D, and E) and reabsorbing B_{12}. The remaining vitamins need to be provided by the diet on a regular basis. A well-balanced diet, containing a wide variety of different foods, is the best way to get all the vitamins you need. Vitamins can be divided into two groups: *water-soluble* (B complex and C) and *fat-soluble* (A, D, and E). Water-soluble vitamins are easily destroyed during cooking, preparing, processing, and storing food. Fat-soluble vitamins are less vulnerable to losses by cooking and processing.

• **Vitamin A** (retinol) is essential for healthy vision, eyes, skin, and growth. Good sources include butter, cheese, cream, eggs, fortified margarine, fortified milk, and liver. The body can convert *beta-carotene*, the yellow-orange pigment found in many colored fruits and vegetables, into vitamin A. In addition to acting as a source of vitamin A, beta-carotene plays an important role as an antioxidant in the body. The best sources of beta-carotene include broccoli, spinach and other dark green leafy vegetables, deep orange fruits (apricots and cantaloupe), and vegetables (carrots, squash, and sweet potatoes).

• **The B Complex vitamins** have very similar roles to play in nutrition, and many of them occur together in the same foods.

Vitamin B_1 (thiamin) is essential in the release of energy from carbohydrates. The best sources include legumes, liver, whole-grain or enriched breads and cereals, nuts, and pork products.

Vitamin B_2 (riboflavin) is vital for growth, healthy skin and eyes, and helps release energy from food. Good sources include cottage cheese, meat, milk, leafy green vegetables, whole-grain or enriched breads and cereals, and yogurt.

Niacin (nicotinic acid), sometimes called vitamin B_3, plays an important role in releasing energy within the cells. Unlike the other B vitamins, the body can make niacin from the essential amino acid *tryptophan*. Good sources include eggs, fish, meats, milk, poultry, whole-grain and enriched breads and cereals, nuts, and all protein-containing foods.

Vitamin B_6 (pyridoxine) helps the body to utilize protein and contributes to the formation of hemoglobin for red blood cells. B_6 is found in fish, fruits, whole grains, legumes, poultry, shellfish, and green leafy vegetables.

Vitamin B_{12} (cyanocobalamin) is vital for growth, the formation of red blood cells, and maintenance of a healthy nervous system. B_{12} is unique in that it is only found in foods of animal origin. Vegetarians who eat dairy products will get enough, but vegans need to include foods fortified with B_{12} in their diet. Good sources of B_{12} include animal products such as cheese, eggs, fish, meat, milk, poultry, and shellfish.

Folate (folic acid) is used in DNA synthesis and is important in the formation of new cells. Folate is important in preventing neural tube defects, such as spina bifida and anencephaly; thus the Public Health Service recommends all women of childbearing age who are capable of becoming pregnant take 0.4 milligrams, or 400 micrograms, of folate daily. As a result, the FDA has mandated that grain products be fortified with folate. The recommended folate level can easily be met by eating 5 or more servings of fruits and vegetables daily, especially leafy green vegetables and oranges. Other good sources include legumes, liver, and seeds.

• **Vitamin C** (ascorbic acid) is essential for growth and vital for the formation of collagen (a protein needed for healthy bones, teeth, gums, blood capillaries, and all connective tissue). It plays an important role in the healing of wounds and fractures, and acts as a powerful antioxidant. The best sources include citrus fruits, cabbage, cantaloupe, lettuce, mangoes, papayas, peppers, strawberries, and dark green vegetables.

• **Vitamin D** (cholecalciferol) is essential for the growth and absorption of calcium, and thus for the formation of healthy bones. Upon exposure to sunlight, the body can synthesize vitamin D. Good food sources include fortified products such as butter, cereals, margarine, and milk.

• **Vitamin E** is not just one vitamin, but a number of related compounds called tocopherols, which function as antioxidants. Good sources of polyunsaturated plant oils and their products include margarine, mayonnaise, salad dressings, and shortenings, plus egg yolks, fortified cereals, liver, nuts, seeds (especially sunflower seeds) leafy green vegetables, and whole-grain products.

Index

A

Alcohol 6, 51
Allicin 141
Almonds
  baked almond-stuffed peaches 108, *109*
  Persian almond crème *136*, 137
Amino acids 141
Antioxidants 10, 32, 34, 48, 59, 62, 65, 72, 82, 84, 90, 94, 108, 126, 132, 138, 140
Apple *10, 11*, 12, 14, *14, 15*, 22
  baked raisin-stuffed 108
  cheese dip, spicy date, and *42*, 43
  crème brûlée, ruby 104
  flambéed, with orange 82
  frijoles with fruit 76, *77*
  in crème caramel 128, *129*
  orchard spread 40, *41*
  pudding autumn 126
  salad, and date 52, *53*
  salsa, date, and orange 43
  shortbread, and blackberry 117
Apricot *10*, 12, *13*, 14, *15*, 22, *23*
  Basque roasted roots 74
  beef and apricot stew 67
  chicken with, and cumin *64*, 65
  Far Eastern roasted roots (dried) 74
  fresh -berry smoothie 28
  golden granola (dried) 44
  hot soufflés 86, *87*
  in chicken with black bean sauce 65
  lamb and, stew (dried) 67
  -pecan muffins 38, *39*
  prune and prosciutto kebabs with sauce 70, *71*
  queen of puddings 114
  roasted roots with (dried) 74, *75*
Asian pear 18, *19*
  flambéed with orange 82, *83*
  pork chops with, 68, *69*

B

Banana 10, *10, 11*, 12, 14, *15*, 22, *23*
  glazed, with pain perdu 92, *93*
  -nut muffins 38
  rice pudding with cranberry *96*, 97
  shake, -berry 32
  shake, with mango 32, *33*
  shake, with peach 32
  smoothie, -berry 28
Beans
  frijoles with fruit 76, *77*
  Mexican lentils with fruit 76
Beef
  Thai stir-fried steak with mango 72, *73*
  Tropical Thai, stir-fry 72

Berry coulis (uncooked) 25, *25*
Berry 12, *13*, 14-16, 22
  in frozen slush with pineapple *36*, 37
  jelly, -red wine 137
  salad with fresh peach sauce 48
  salad with passion fruit 48, *49*
  slush, three-berry 37
  summer pudding 126, *127*
  sundae, fresh 48
Beta-carotene 6, 10, *11, 13*, 51, 54, 59, 65, 72, 74, 89, 141
Bioflavonoids 10, *10*, 94, 141
Black Forest mousse cake 122, *123*
Blackberry *13*, 14, *15*, 16
  coulis (cooked) 25, *25*
  granita 134
  phyllo pizzas, with peach 94, *95*
  sauce, fresh 100
  shortbread, with apple 117
  with apple crème caramel 128, *129*
  yogurt, frozen 131
Black currant *11*, 12, 14, *15*, 16
Blueberry 12, *13, 15*, 16, 22, *23*
  granola, and cranberry 44, *45*
  muffins, fresh, -nut 38
  shortbread, pear and *116*, 117
Bread
  Autumn pudding 126
  pain perdu, glazed banana 92, *93*
  queen of puddings, raspberry 114, *115*
  summer pudding 126, *127*
Breakfast fruits (a great start) 26-45
Brochettes, grilled fruit 84, *85*
Bulghur 70

C

Cactus (prickly) pear 18, *19*
Cake, Black Forest mousse 122, *123*
Calcium 7, 32, 54, 78, 90, 97, 98, 100, 106, 110, 112, 137, 141
Calories 6, 140
Cape gooseberry 18, *19*
Carambola (star fruit) 18, *18*
Carbohydrate 7, 97, 140
Carotenoids 32, 141
Cheese 7
  dip, spicy date, apple and *42*, 43
  in filling for strawberry tart 120, *121*
  nectarines grilled with gorgonzola 78
  pears broiled with pecorino 78, *79*
  raspberries with grilled brie 78
  salad, pear and gorgonzola 54
  salad, watermelon and feta 54, *55*
Cheesecake
  apricot 125
  berry 125
  sour cherry 125
  sultana lemon *124*, 125

Cherry *10*, 16, *16*, 22, *23*
  Black Forest mousse cake 122, *123*
  cheesecake, sour cherry 125
  clafoutis, brandy 110, *111*
  clafoutis, sugar 'n' spice 110
  fool, Bing 98
  granola, -berry 44
  pears, baked, -stuffed 108
  -rice pudding, creamy 97
Chicken
  apricot, with black bean sauce 65
  Asian 69
  cutlets with fresh oranges 65
  Thai stir-fried chicken with nectarines 72
  with apricots and cumin *64*, 65
Chloride 141
Chocolate
  Black Forest mousse cake 122, *123*
  in sauce with pear crêpes 106, *107*
  raspberry Black Forest mousse cake 122
  raspberry queen of puddings 114, *115*
Cholesterol 62, 76, 92, 122, 140
Chromium 141
Citrus and spinach salad *58*, 59
Citrus, spinach and gorgonzola salad 59
Citrus fruit *11*, 12, *13*, 16, 34
Citrus pain perdu 93
Citrus wake-up 34, *35*
Clafoutis
  cherry brandy 110, *111*
  red grape 110
Clementine, in plums *en papillote* 90
Copper 10, 141
Coulis 25
  berry (uncooked) 25, *25*
  berry, with raspberry crêpes 106
  blackberry (cooked) 25, *25*
  raspberry-orange 84, *85*
Cranberry *15*, 16, 22, *23*
  crème brûlée 104
  granita, strawberry and 134, *135*
  granola, blueberry and 44, *45*
  rice pudding, banana and *96*, 97
Crème anglaise 112, *113*
Crème brûlée
  cranberry 104
  rhubarb and saffron 104, *105*
  ruby apple 104
Crème caramel, apple 128, *129*
Crème fraîche, mock 118, 122, 126, *127*
Currant 12, *13*, 14, *15*, 22, *23*
Custard apple 19, *19*
Custards, Spanish orange 128

D

Dairy foods 7
Daily Value (DV) 140
Damson 17, *17*

index

Date 12, *13,* 19, *19,* 22, *23,* 43, 52
    dip, spicy, apple, and cheese *42,* 43
    salad, apple and 52, *53*
    salsa, apple, and orange 43
Desserts, fast fruit 80-101
Dietary Guidelines for Americans 6, 140
Dressings, salad
    balsamic 59
    chili and coriander 56
    lemon 54
    vinaigrette 52
    yogurt 52
Dried fruit *10, 11,* 22, *23,* 38, 40
    concentrated fruity goodness 22-23, *22-23*
    granola, blueberry and cranberry 44, *45*
    orange cranberry spread 40
    orchard spread 40, *41*
    mixed fruit spread 40
drinks 28-37

E

Eggs 7, 104, 122
    crème brûlée 104, *105*
    crème caramel, apple 128, *129*
    pain perdu, glazed banana *92,* 93
Essential fatty acids 140
Exercise 6
Exotic fruits 12, 18-21, *18-21*

F

Fat 7, 67, 69, 90, 122, 140
Fabulous fruits for a healthy diet 10-13, *10-13*
Favorite fruits, a new look at 14-17, *14-17*
Feijoa 19, *19*
Fiber 7, 12, 23, 140
Fig *19,* 19, 22, *23*
    stew, lamb and, with star anise 66, *67*
Flowers, edible *50,* 51
Folate 34, 140, 142
Food Guide Pyramid 6-7, *7,* 140
Fool, summer fruit 98, *99*
Free radicals 6, 140
Fruit, grilled
    en brochettes 84, 85
    saffron and vanilla *88,* 89
    summer 89
    tropical 89
Fruits from around the world 18-21, *18-21*

G

Glucose 140
Glucosinolates 141
Glycemic Index (GI) 23, 140
Gooseberry *15,* 16
Granadilla 21
Granita, strawberry and cranberry 134, *135*
Grapefruit *11, 13,* 16, *58,* 59
Granola 44, *45*

Grape *10,* 14, 16, *16*
    red grape clafoutis 110
Greengage 17, *17*
Guava 12, *13,* 19, *19*

I, J, K

Ice cream
    fresh peach 138
    sweet balsamic berry 138, *139*
Iron 7, 10, *11,* 17, 44, 140, 141
Isoflavones 141
Jelly, berry red-wine 137
Kiwi 7, *11,* 12, *13,* 17, 20, *20,* 34
    fruit market salad 56
    minted tropical fruit salad 56
    tropical fruit with coriander 56, *57*
Kumquat *16,* 16
    steamed kumquat honey pudding 112, *113*

L

Lamb and fig stew with star anise 66, *67*
Lemon *10, 13,* 16, *16*
    cheesecake, sultana *124,* 125
    fool, lemony plum 98
Lime *10, 13, 14,* 16, *16*
Litchi (lychee) 12, 20, *20*
Loganberry 14
Lycopene 76, 141

M

Magnesium 140, 141
Mandarin 16
Mango *11,* 12, 20, *20,* 22, *23*
    fizz, peach and apricot *30,* 31
    in tropical slush 37
    shake, banana and 32, *33*
    with stir-fried steak, Thai-style 72, *73*
Melon *10, 11,* 12, *16,* 17, *17*
    Pimm's melon cup *50,* 51
Mexican fruit gazpacho 34
Mexican lentils with fruit 76
Milk 7, 32, 97, 106, 110, 112
    Persian almond crème *136,* 137
    rhubarb and saffron crème brûlée 104, *105*
Minerals 6, 10, 24, 140, 141
Monounsaturated fats 140
Muffins
    apricot–pecan 38, *39*
    banana-nut 38
    fresh blueberry-nut 38
    fresh peach 38
    fresh strawberry 38

N

Nectarine 14, *15*
    baked cranberry-stuffed 108
    grilled with gorgonzola 78
    kebabs, turkey and 70

    phyllo pizzas, and raspberry 95
    shortbread, and raspberry 117
    with Thai stir-fried chicken 72
Niacin 140, 141
Nuts 7, 117, 118
    granola, honey- 44

O

Orange 7, *11, 13,* 16, *16,* 83
    chicken cutlets with fresh 65
    citrus wake-up 34, *35*
    coulis, raspberry and 84, *84*
    crêpes, fresh 106
    custards, Spanish 128
    granita, fresh 134
    in flambéed Asian pears 82, *83*
    in scallop sauté 62
    Mexican fruit gazpacho 34
    summery sparkler 34
Orchard spread 40, *41*
Organic fruit 12

P

Pain perdu, glazed banana *92,* 93
Papaya *10, 11,* 12, *13,* 20, *20,* 22, *23*
Passion fruit 12, *13,* 20, 21
    in berry salad 48, *49*
Peach *10, 11,* 12, *13,* 14, *15,* 22, *23,* 94, 108
    baked almond-stuffed 108, *109*
    clafoutis, fresh 110
    fizz, mango, and apricot *30,* 31
    ice cream, fresh 138
    muffins, fresh 38
    pastry pockets 118
    phyllo pizzas, with blackberry 94, *95*
    sauce, fresh, with berry salad 48
    sauce, no-cook 100
    slush, rosy 37
    spread, vanilla 40
    tart, raspberry- 120
    trifle 132
    yogurt, frozen 131
Pear 12, 17, *17,* 22, *23*
    baked cherry-stuffed 108
    Comice, flambéed with orange 82
    crêpes with chocolate sauce 106, *107*
    broiled with pecorino 78, *79*
    in pastry pockets 118
    phyllo pizzas, with raspberry 95
    shortbread, with blueberry *116,* 117
    see also Asian pear
Persian almond crème *136,* 137
Persimmon 18, 21, *21*
Phyllo pastry
    nectarine and raspberry pizzas 95
    peach and blackberry pizzas 94, *95*
    peach pastry pockets 118
    pear and raspberry pizzas 95

pear pastry pockets 118
plum and marzipan pastries 118, *119*
plum and raspberry pizzas 95
Phytochemicals 6, 141
Phytoestrogens 141
Pimm's melon cup *50,* 51
Pineapple 12, *13, 20,* 21, 22, *23*
flambéed with orange 82
en papillote, fresh, with banana 90
in frijoles with fruit 76, *77*
in frozen slush, with berry *36,* 37
in spicy fish satay 62
Thai shrimp and 62, *63*
Plum 12, 17, *17*
hot sauce 100, *101*
plum and marzipan pastries 118, *119*
en papillote with clementines 90
en papillote with honey 90, *91*
toffee papillotes 90
Polyunsaturated fats 140
Pomegranate 21, *21*
Pork
chops with Asian pears 68, *69*
Mediterraneanné 69
Potassium 10, *11,* 12, 32, 40, 140, 141
Preparing and cooking fruits 24-25, *24-25*
Prickly pear 18, *19*
Prosciutto and prune kebabs 70, *71*
Protein 6, 7, 69, 86, 117, 141
Prune 22, 23, *23*
in prosciutto kebabs with apricot sauce 70, *71*

Q

Queen of puddings
cinnamon 'n' spice 114
fresh apricot 114
raspberry 114, *115*
Quercetin 141
Quince *20,* 21

R

Raisins 23, *23*
baked, -stuffed apples 108
golden, in cinnamon rice pudding 97
in cinnamon swirl pain perdu 92
Rambutan *20,* 21
Raspberry 12, *13,* 14, *15,* 16
crêpes 106
hot soufflés 86
in berry coulis (uncooked) 25, *25*
in chocolate mousse cake 122
-orange coulis 84, *85*
phyllo pizzas, with nectarine 95
queen of puddings 114, *115*
-rice pudding 97
shortbread, with nectarine 117
-strawberry granita 134

tart, -peach 120
trifle 132
with grilled brie 78
yogurt, frozen *130,* 131
Raw vitality (salads with fruit) 46-59
Rhubarb 17, *17,* 104
crème brûlée, and saffron 104, *105*
Rice pudding
cranberry and banana *96,* 97
creamy cherry- 97
raspberry- 97
Root vegetables
roasted roots with apricots 74, *75*

S

Saffron and vanilla grilled fruit *88,* 89
Salads 46-59
apple and date 52, *53*
berry, with passion fruit 48, *49*
citrus and spinach *58,* 59
Pimm's cup *50,* 51
tropical fruit with coriander 56, *57*
watermelon and feta salad 54, *55*
Salt 6
Satsuma 16
Saturated fatty acids 140
Savory and spicy ways with fruit 60-78
Seeds 54, 140
Selenium 10, 62, 141
Sharon fruit 21, *21*
Shrimp, Thai, and pineapple 62, *63*
Sodium 6, 54, 128, 141
Sorbet, fruit 134
Soufflés
fresh strawberry 86
hot apricot 86, *87*
hot raspberry 86
Spanish orange custards 128, *129*
Spinach salad with fruits
with citrus *58,* 59
with citrus and gorgonzola 59
zesty 59
Star fruit (carambola) 18, *18*
Strawberry *11,* 12, *13,* 14, *15,* 16, 17, 132
fool, fresh 98
granita, and cranberry 134, *135*
in cheese tart 120, *121*
in sorbet 134
in Black Forest mousse cake 122
muffins, fresh 38
sea island tart 120
slush, frozen pineapple and berry 37
smoothie, yogurt 28, *29*
trifle 132
yogurt, frozen 131
Sugars 6, 52, 140
Sulforaphane 141

Sulfur 141
Sultana 23
lemon cheesecake *124,* 125
Summer fruit fool 98, *99*
Summer pudding 126, *127*
Super fruit 8-25
Sweet balsamic berry ice cream 138, *139*
Sweet finales 102-139

T

Tamarillo 18, 21, *21*
Tart, strawberry cheese 120, *121*
Thai
shrimp and pineapple 62, *63*
stir-fried chicken with nectarines 72
stir-fried steak with mango 72, *73*
Tomato *76*
Trace minerals 141
Trans fats 140
Trifle, tropical 132, *133*
Tropical fruit
an ABC of 18-21
with coriander 56, *57*

U, V, W

Unsaturated fatty acids 140
Vegetarian stew 67
Vitamins 10-12, *13,* 17, 24, 141-142
Watermelon 17, *17*
and feta salad 54, *55*

Y, Z

Yogurt 7, 24, 28, 52, 90, 98
blackberry, frozen 131
in strawberry smoothie 28, *29*
in summer fruit fool 98, *99*
raspberry, frozen *130,* 131
strawberry, frozen 131
Zinc 10, 140, 141

index

144